HIGH-IMPACT LEADERSHIP IN CATHOLIC EDUCATION

HIGH-IMPACT LEADERSHIP IN CATHOLIC EDUCATION

JUDITH A. DWYER

Georgetown University Press / Washington, DC

© 2024 Judith A Dwyer. All rights reserved. No part of this book may be reproduced or utilized in any form or by any means, electronic or mechanical, including photocopying and recording, or by any information storage and retrieval system, without permission in writing from the publisher.

The publisher is not responsible for third-party websites or their content. URL links were active at time of publication.

Cataloging-in-Publication Data is on file with the Library of Congress.

ISBN 978-1-64712-461-8 (hardcover)
ISBN 978-1-64712-462-5 (paperback)
ISBN 978-1-64712-463-2 (ebook)

∞ This paper meets the requirements of ANSI/NISO Z39.48-1992 (Permanence of Paper).

25 24   9 8 7 6 5 4 3 2 First printing

Printed in the United States of America

Cover design by Nathan Putens
Interior design by Paul Hotvedt

In memory of my parents,
James P. Dwyer and Mary E. Dwyer

TABLE OF CONTENTS

	Introduction	1
1	The Centrality of the Mission	8
2	The Strategic Plan as Institutional Road Map	25
3	Fostering a Vibrant Community	48
4	Risk Assessment and Crisis Management	75
5	Governance	95
6	Qualities of High-Impact Leadership	115
	Conclusion	132
	Bibliography	*135*
	Index	*143*
	About the Author	*149*

Introduction

ROM ONE GENERATION TO THE NEXT, Catholic K-12 schools, colleges, and universities have educated students throughout the United States and the world, testifying to the belief that the quest for truth is inextricably linked to the quest for God. These schools, scattered around the globe, have long recognized the authenticity of faith-based education in which all aspects of the whole person—intellectual, physical, psychological, social, and spiritual—are understood to be deeply interrelated, even as students are challenged to develop and grow. From a simple building in a remote village within a developing country to a sprawling urban university campus, this ecclesial mission continues today.

How does one become a leader of a Catholic academic community in our contemporary situation? What responsibilities are involved? What qualities are needed, and how are they achieved? What characterizes the type of community that can support the Catholic mission? This book is designed to address these questions and serve as a resource for administrators within Catholic schools (K-12 parochial and independent schools, colleges, and universities). Throughout the book the title "president" refers to a school's chief executive officer, head of school, head teacher, superintendent, or any similar role that denotes the highest level of authority in the school or the individual who has ultimate responsibility for the school's success. While experienced presidents will recognize the leadership role and

2 Introduction

responsibilities presented, this book is explicitly designed for those new to a presidency or those who aspire to that role, including provosts, vice presidents, deans, department chairs, and program directors. In addition, this work can serve as an essential resource for boards of trustees and those charged with the responsibility of selecting an academic community's president.

"School" is used as a comprehensive term to include K-12 parochial and independent schools and colleges and universities, as the strategic principles articulated here apply to all areas of Catholic education, even though the contexts are exceptionally varied and numerous. While some may balk at the application of key strategic principles across the broad spectrum of the K-12 and higher education levels, educators can gain valuable insights concerning leadership from colleagues who serve at multiple educational levels within this complex academic world.

The term "board of trustees" represents all roles at the highest level of responsibility in terms of governance. Depending on a school's structure and context, this highest level of governance may be a diocesan bishop, a sponsoring religious community, or a board of trustees dominated by laywomen and laymen. All models and structures of governance authority are encompassed in the term.[1]

This study is not a history of Catholic education in a particular country, including the United States, nor does it specifically focus on recognized leaders within Catholic education's distinguished history. There is no in-depth analysis of the impact of papal teachings, such as John Paul II's apostolic constitution "On Catholic Universities."[2] It does not examine various documents on the role of Catholic schools as issued by the United States Conference of Catholic Bishops (USCCB) or individual bishops.[3] These important documents are known to most Catholic school administrators and there are excellent opportunities to study their content and impact provided by the Association of Catholic Colleges and Universities (ACCU) and the National Catholic Educational Association (NCEA).[4] Additionally, this book does not address critical issues that have impacted Catholic

Introduction 3

education for many years, such as academic freedom, the role of the local bishop, the role of the laity, and so forth. While all these issues deserve extensive analysis, other excellent scholarly materials do exist that provide that very justified attention.[5]

The scope of this book is more modest: it is a gathering of all the factors, functions, duties, and requirements that make up the world of a president in a Catholic academic institution. Here I take a panoramic perspective rather than provide an in-depth exploration of leadership responsibilities that might entail—by way of example—very detailed templates for strategic planning or specific programs or tools that conduct risk assessments. The focus here is overarching: What functions and responsibilities are required of a Catholic school leader, and what leadership qualities allow one to successfully achieve these duties and obligations? As Peter F. Drucker has frequently noted, "Executives are doers; they execute."[6] What levels of competencies are required of all presidents to execute this role successfully? What are the core qualities and skills required of those who seek efficiency, effectiveness, high levels of academic achievement, and fresh perspectives on their role as thought leaders and change agents? Why is high-impact leadership essential to realizing a successful, dynamic Catholic school, and how can presidents in the academic world draw from a wide range of resources to enhance their own development as leaders?

The high-impact president exhibits specific approaches, principles, and qualities that achieve significant strategic goals within a concise time frame; these traits have both an immediate and a long-term impact on the institution. In addition, high-impact leadership situates the Catholic school's mission and strategic plan as the foundation and framework for addressing the many tactical issues that comprise the daily life of a school community.

High-impact leaders think and act in a nimble, adaptive manner and hold strategic and tactical issues in creative tension. They embrace tight deadlines even as they commit to a consultative, community-based way of leading. They take risks without

4   *Introduction*

being reckless; they pursue excellence but not elitism; they prefer simple solutions but are not simplistic in their decision-making.

As a result, high-impact leaders promote their schools' Catholic mission and foster a vibrant community; engage their students, faculty, and staff; execute robust strategic plans; empower student leadership; create innovative campus master plans; oversee significant construction projects; address pressing legal issues (often relating to personnel matters); shape a sustainable financial model; mentor senior leadership teams; foster effective governance with a board of trustees; successfully engage their alumni and communities; and generate philanthropic support—an array of responsibilities that exist simultaneously and require constant balance, frequent reprioritization, and successful, timely fulfillment.

While most presidents are innately inclined to select processes and programs that are best for their schools, the purpose here is to offer practical recommendations and a series of questions that encourage further reflection concerning administrative approaches and choices. The questions raised are illustrative and not meant to be comprehensive. For additional consideration, a case study appears at the end of each chapter. These case studies do not recount any real situation or event in any school where I served as a faculty member or administrator, except the case study presented in chapter 4, Risk Assessment and Crisis Management. I have altered many details of that very public case about which I wrote at the time.[7] The other fictional case studies illustrate specific "tension points" that may occasionally be found within an academic community.

Throughout the text, references are periodically made to great twentieth- and twenty-first-century leaders who demonstrated high-impact leadership in various fields and whose lives can be viewed as a whole, offering inspiration through the complete arc of a well-lived life. My hope is that presidents and anyone who aspires to a leadership role in education will seriously

Introduction 5

consider these historical models as important mentors—and do so to enhance their own present-day presidential success.

I have been privileged to explore the topic of educational leadership in discussions with Lincoln Snyder, president/CEO of the NCEA, who shared keen insights concerning K-12 parochial and independent schools. Conversations with Rev. Dennis H. Holtschneider, CM, EdD, the president of the ACCU, also offered important observations about Catholic higher education's challenges and opportunities in the twenty-first century. Rev. Thomas P. Gaunt, SJ, PhD, the executive director of the Center for Applied Research in the Apostolate (CARA) at Georgetown University, suggested topics for additional research and helpfully referenced important information concerning national education statistics. Dr. Andrew M. McLaughlin, the secretary of elementary education for the Archdiocese of Philadelphia, thoughtfully discussed trends in K-8 education, and Dr. Samuel J. Levy, former vice president for information resources and technologies at the University of St. Thomas (in Saint Paul, Minnesota), offered helpful insights concerning state-of-the-art learning commons. Bob Regan, senior consultant of Catholic schools practice at Carney, Sandoe & Associates, kindly shared reflections on his important monograph on leadership in Catholic schools and graciously offered ideas concerning best practices in financial matters.

Joan Stahl, director of research and instruction at the University Libraries of Catholic University of America, thoughtfully assisted this alumna in research requests, and Catholic University graduate student Micaela Champion served as my research assistant during the final phases of this project. In addition, I thank Gwynedd Mercy University's Dr. Lisa McGarry, dean of the School of Arts and Sciences, who extended valuable access to her institution's university library. Cindy Moon-Barna, the director of the library at the Council for Advancement and Support of Education (CASE), suggested important resources. I thank Al Bertrand, the director of Georgetown University Press,

6 *Introduction*

for his support of this project, and his entire staff, who have also been exceptionally helpful throughout this process.

All these collegial conversations, along with invaluable research and administrative and publishing assistance, only deepened my appreciation of those who have generously dedicated their professional careers to strengthening the field of education. For this reason I express my deep gratitude to all the outstanding students, faculty members, staff, and trustees with whom I have been honored to work throughout my career in Catholic education; their untiring efforts faithfully fulfill the Catholic Church's educational mission.

Leading any school is a complex task but also a great privilege. It is a role that holds a unique sphere of influence and authority within a school community. While this responsibility challenges the president on a daily basis, it also presents the president with opportunities to exercise genuine courage, compassion, healing, mentorship, and vision. Moreover, in committing to lead a Catholic school, the president advances the centuries-old belief that education in a faith-based environment remains the best frontier for new possibilities and builds a context that creates a future of immeasurable hope and promise.

Notes

1. For the canonical role of the bishop in relationship to Catholic schools, see *Code of Canon Law*, Canons 794, 803 #1 and #3, cited in NCEA, *National Standards and Benchmarks*, 10.
2. Pope John Paul II, *Apostolic Constitution on Catholic Universities.* See also Pope Benedict XVI, Address to Catholic Educators; Congregation for Catholic Education, *Identity of the Catholic School*; Congregation for Catholic Education, *The Catholic School*; Congregation for Catholic Education, *Educating Together*; and Pontifical Council for the Promotion of the New Evangelization, *Directory for Catechesis.*
3. USCCB, *To Teach*; USCCB, *Renewing Our Commitment*; Miller, *Holy See's Teaching.*
4. See the websites of the ACCU (https://accunet.org) and the NCEA (https://ncea.org).

Introduction   7

5. For example, see Heft, *Future of Catholic Higher Education*; Morey and Piderit, *Catholic Higher Education*; Gleason, *Contending with Modernity*; and Breen and Strang, "Academic Freedom."
6. Drucker, "What Makes an Effective Executive," 60.
7. Dwyer, "Preparing for the Unthinkable."

1

The Centrality of the Mission

THE MISSION OF A CATHOLIC SCHOOL reflects its very reason for being. Rooted in deep faith and moral values, embraced by the present and committed to shaping the future, a Catholic school's mission endures and inspires even as its articulation, understanding, and implementation evolve over time. Motivated by the example of Jesus Christ and the Church's two-thousand-year practice of uniting faith and reason, this mission often reflects the charism of a founding religious community or the spirit of the diocese that established the school at some point in time, thereby committing itself to education and the realization of this serious ecclesial duty.

While every member of a school community has responsibility for understanding and promoting the school's mission, presidents have a unique role and privileged opportunity to teach the community about the mission and its succinct articulation through the school's mission statement. It is incumbent on presidents to stress the centrality of the mission in the life of the Catholic academic community, and to accomplish this unique role leaders must know their school's mission and the distinctive history and traditions that have sustained that mission. However, they must also believe in this mission. There must be genuine energy when they speak about their school's mission. It must be clear to the audience (students and their parents, faculty, staff, trustees, alumni, and the wider community) that their leader understands the school's mission, embraces this mission, and is committed to realizing its ongoing impact within the organization.

In addition to presenting the mission as the foundation of a Catholic school's identity, the president must also stress the inclusive nature of all Catholic academic communities. Catholic schools have welcomed students from all faiths, all races, all cultures, and all economic spheres—and have done so for generations. By way of example, the history of Catholic education in the United States, including the present day, is a significant testimony to the Church's deep commitment to educating all immigrant communities, with special attention to the poor and all who are marginalized in any way.[1] Likewise, Catholic school administrators, faculty, and staff often reflect diverse religious backgrounds, even as these individuals respect the Catholic faith and values that distinguish the academic community in which they work. This diversity can significantly enrich the vibrant nature of the school, fostering a culture of genuine respect while never diminishing its authentic Catholic nature.[2]

Promoting the Mission

What does it mean to be an academic community deeply rooted in a life of faith? Why does Pope John Paul II describe a Catholic university as "born from the heart of the Church," an "incomparable center of creativity and dissemination of knowledge for the good of humanity?"[3] By reverently holding the school's mission before the eyes of varied constituencies in a concise and focused way, a president demonstrates that the mission is an essential dimension of the Church's identity and the foundation for the school's very existence.

One key to connecting the centrality of mission to the community is to make intentional "mission links" with day-to-day school activities—in academics, admissions, alumni engagement, athletics, facilities management, finances, fundraising, information resources/technologies, marketing/communications, and student life. These connections testify that the mission is

10   *Chapter 1*

alive and well throughout the daily life of the academic community. Many specific moments throughout the academic year, such as Eucharistic celebrations, student retreats, interdisciplinary theology seminars—or environmental research in which a faculty member may be engaged—can offer authentic opportunities for this "mission link."

The mission is also alive and well through service opportunities that promote the enduring power of Catholic social teaching within the academic community, that is, belief in the inherent sacredness of human life, deep respect for human dignity, a commitment to community and promoting the common good, and an understanding that there is no authentic peace without justice, to cite a few principles.[4] By promoting the common good, unity, and the healing of broken relationships, these fundamental moral values provide an important alternative and practical framework to address the serious ideological shifts that currently fragment our culture. The critical point is that the president has a wealth of examples from which to draw these mission links and multiple opportunities to make this vital connection—whether in formal speeches, weekly updates, town hall meetings with students or faculty, or written communications to parents, alumni, or trustees.

However, some presidents may fear they reference the mission statement too much. They frequently hesitate to allude to the mission in their communications, believing that the audience "has already heard it." Usually the opposite is true: too many leaders do not sufficiently reference their schools' missions and squander opportunities to teach their communities about their missions' vitality, relevance to the present, and promise for the future. A president must always remember that the school's constituencies, with their many responsibilities, communications, and distractions, do not usually live their daily lives focused on their school's mission. In addition, leaders speak to different groups at different times. The message may be very familiar to the leader but much less so to the audience. By using the office of the presidency to promote the school's mission, administrators can exercise their unique role by reminding the community of the very reason for the school's existence. While the broader school community may not initially appreciate it, the president also knows that the school's mission establishes the foundation for its strategic planning, shapes programs and rituals within the community, impacts personnel decisions, influences investment decisions, and assists in attracting donors. When done properly, this integration of the mission into most of the president's communications will seem neither forced nor artificial.

In addition to formal communications by the school president, there are manifold ways to promote the centrality of the mission. These include displaying the mission statement on the school's webpage and throughout its promotional materials as well as posting the mission statement throughout the campus (and not simply in the administrative corridor). It is highly effective to have every building, including residence halls, display this powerful statement in their entrances or lobbies, reminding all who pass by that the central values articulated in the school's mission should permeate the daily life and work of all students, faculty, and staff.

In addition to placing the mission statement in key campus locations, it is also important that the Catholic school's physical spaces reflect its identity as a faith-based community and include the presence of an attractive, well-maintained, centrally located chapel. Catholicism is a religion of mediation, that is, it holds the belief that God's love manifests itself in multiple ways—most significantly in the person of Jesus Christ but also through the Sign of the Cross, the beauty of art and music, the symbolic power of water and oil, the inspiring lives of the saints, the gift of a vibrant community's support, and the preciousness of our fragile world. In centrally situating the chapel and placing religious symbols tastefully throughout the campus, the school speaks to this centuries-old theological tradition, and a visitor to the school should experience an environment that embodies this cherished legacy.

12   *Chapter 1*

Office of Mission/Campus Ministry

While the president of a Catholic school community holds the primary responsibility to foster the school's mission, most leaders establish an Office of Mission or Campus Ministry (or similar title) to plan and coordinate all efforts in creating a vibrant, mission-focused community. Among its many responsibilities, this office oversees the school chapel and coordinates a rich liturgical life for the community, particularly with celebrations of the Eucharist and Sacrament of Reconciliation.

The frequent celebration of the Eucharist speaks to the priority of the Catholic faith in the life of the academic community and liturgies are unique moments to empower students, faculty, and staff to exercise leadership in all planning and participation, including the reverent (and prepared) reading of the Scriptures and Prayers of the Faithful and service as musicians or Eucharistic ministers. Special occasions such as the Mass of the Holy Spirit to begin the academic year, a School Ring Mass before senior year, or a Baccalaureate Mass at graduation are opportunities to gather the community in unique moments of celebration. In addition, important days such as All Saints, Ash Wednesday, and Ascension Thursday usually occur when school is in session, presenting opportunities to celebrate the richness of the liturgical life with the entire campus.

Ideally a Catholic school community comes together for Eucharistic celebrations regularly, and the Sacrament of Reconciliation is made regularly available, especially during the liturgical seasons of Advent and Lent. In addition to these sacramental celebrations, campus-wide weekly community prayer gatherings offer a specific time and place to hear God's Word and reflect and express gratitude for God's many gifts. These gatherings demonstrate that a life of prayer is a priority for the school community and an essential way it lives its mission.

The importance of liturgical and prayerful gatherings cannot be underestimated.[5] Alumni often wonder whether their alma mater still regularly celebrates Mass or offers special Advent

The Centrality of the Mission   13

programs for students. It is not unusual for many graduates to express their fond recollections of these moments from their past, grateful in the knowledge that these mission-focused celebrations are still an essential part of the school's life.

The Office of Mission/Campus Ministry is also responsible for hosting student, faculty, and staff retreats, providing focused opportunities to reflect on the ongoing commitment to a life of prayer, especially during Advent and Lent. In our fast-paced world, drenched by constant bombardment from social media, these reflective moments especially touch the deeper aspects of a student's experience, providing time that is not saturated by the unrelenting noise of today's society. Such designated times for prayer and reflection offer an oasis from the "globalization of superficiality" that today surrounds young people on a 24/7 basis.[6] These opportunities challenge students "to continue to search for truth and meaning throughout their lives" and provide moments to cultivate the ability to wonder, understand, contemplate, make personal decisions, and develop a religious, moral, and social sense.[7]

Many retreats offer important leadership opportunities for students as well, demonstrating that peers' reflections on the spiritual life are often one of the more compelling and impactful aspects of such gatherings. Moreover, retreats offered by the local diocese or sponsoring religious community present a broader context for students, faculty, and staff to step away in quiet prayer from the unrelenting pace of today's world, which is increasingly overwhelmed with information that is often transmitted devoid of wisdom or a critical sense.[8]

Carefully planned service experiences that partner academic community members with existing social outreach programs also testify to the school's deep commitment to the Catholic mission. By employing a cycle of study, direct service, and reflection, the school can commit to preparations on issues addressed by a specific group or organization (for example, hunger or illiteracy), followed by direct service at the site itself and subsequent reflection on the experience. For those who serve in the

14   *Chapter 1*

role of the president (and campus ministers), it is essential to understand and integrate these experiences by explicitly linking the service to the school's mission and the social teachings of the Catholic Church as "the joy and hope, the grief and anguish of the men [and women] of our time, especially those who are poor or afflicted in any way, are the joy and hope, the grief and anguish of the followers of Christ as well."[9] What does human dignity mean in the context of grief and anguish? Why does the Catholic faith believe in the intrinsic value of every human life? Why is feeding the poor and caring for the homeless an essential element of the Catholic faith's embrace of human pain? Why does the Catholic faith prioritize caring for the sick and dying? Why is this environmental project related to the concept of a "common home," as Pope Francis often describes our fragile world?[10] Service-learning opportunities are more than opportunities for humanitarian outreach; instead, they reflect the important mission-related responsibilities relevant to all areas of life.[11] Making this specific mission link is a critical step, as it should not be assumed that this connection is apparent to all participants or readily appreciated for its profundity.

Mission-Related Professional Development Opportunities

Presidents have a special obligation to offer mission-related professional development opportunities regularly for all students and employees (see chapter 3). Topics of focus might include the Church's teaching on the ecclesial mission of education, Catholic social teaching and its relevance in the contemporary world, a history of the founding and evolution of Catholic education or of the school itself, and many others. Presidents should not assume that the faculty, staff, and other administrators have a working knowledge of or background in these areas, even though these topics provide the vital foundation and context for understanding the purpose and mission of Catholic education. The ACCU and the NCEA offer excellent professional development programs that address these areas, as do several Catholic colleges and universities, including Georgetown University, Boston College, and the University of Notre Dame.

To state it directly, presidents have egregiously failed in their role if they do not ensure that mission-related activities (celebrations of the Eucharist and Sacrament of Reconciliation, community prayer, school retreats, service-learning experiences, and mission-related professional development opportunities) are frequently offered and carefully coordinated within their academic communities. While the many planning details of these opportunities are delegated to others, the president must ensure that these religious rituals and experiences remain a significant priority in the community's life. Given time constraints, it is too easy to allow these mission-related experiences to be postponed or slip away entirely. In addition, the president must make every effort to attend these celebrations and community prayer offerings, as this presence speaks to presidential priorities and is noted by community members.

Theology/Religious Studies Departments

The role of a Theology or Religious Studies Department uniquely reflects a school's commitment to the mission by providing a critical opportunity for the substantive study of Catholic identity, its rich intellectual tradition, and its contemporary expression, along with the study of other Christian faiths and world religions.[12] It is the responsibility of the president and other administrators to ensure that these departments meet the standards of rigorous academic work, stay true to their identity, and do not devolve into social studies departments that embrace only political, economic, cultural, or geographic content that is devoid of genuine theological elucidation. On the other hand, a Theology or Religious Studies Department that attempts to proselytize students has seriously failed in its unique role within the intellectual life of a Catholic academic community.

16   *Chapter 1*

Mission Effectiveness

While many formal survey instruments are available to assess a community's active engagement in the mission, other spontaneous and anecdotal moments can capture mission effectiveness best. For instance, one of the greatest joys that a president can experience is to hear a student, in an unprompted moment, speak about the school's mission and do so with confidence and pride. This is a sure sign that students—the center of every school community—have embraced the school's mission; they "own it" and can easily, and without embarrassment, speak to its power. Such experiences testify to the centrality and vibrant nature of the mission, as one generation of students after the next embraces the mission and its power to inspire.

Revising the Mission Statement: A Model for Intentional Collaboration

After a thorough assessment, a school's board of trustees and president may determine that the school's mission needs to be better articulated and more widely known through a revised mission statement. The president must demonstrate that such a revision does not change the school's mission nor does it indicate some radical departure from the school's long-standing cherished values.[13] Moreover, the opportunity to revise the mission statement—how a school describes its mission—does provide a special moment to celebrate the past while reinvigorating, and reemphasizing its present-day and future importance. The mission statement is a "living document," thus neither static nor dated.

This responsibility for reassuring others is vital, because revising the mission statement can be a sensitive topic. There can exist confusion and even fear when a school community announces it will embark on a revision of the mission statement. Is it not unusual to hear many questions: What is wrong with the current mission statement? Is the school changing its

The Centrality of the Mission   17

mission? Has the community abandoned its core values? Does this process violate tradition? These and other queries may arise when communities begin the critical, systematic process of revising the mission statement, and it is therefore imperative that leaders immediately address any confusion or fear that may swirl around within their communities. Leaders must be able to explain, with clarity and deep respect, the necessity of the task and its purpose while also assuring all members of the school community that the school's beliefs and core values are not being jettisoned.

Revising the mission statement is also an opportunity for a president to promote the qualities and characteristics of a strong mission statement. There is no "perfect mission statement." Instead, each school community must develop a statement that fits its community: one that the school can own, one that is clear and authentic, and one that encompasses the whole while realizing the inherent limitations of all words and processes. A strong mission statement should specifically reference the Catholic nature of the school and a faith-filled and intellectual tradition that inspires, energizes, and guides the present while pointing to the future. A forceful mission statement should be brief—no more than one or two sentences—and should distill the essence of the school's reason for being—often described as the "soul" of the institution.

Unfortunately, some Catholic school mission statements do not forthrightly acknowledge the Catholic nature of the institution, as if this reality were something to bury for fear of negative interpretations. Some Catholic schools use more humanitarian terms that, while laudable, could describe any school anywhere. In these cases, presidents have failed in their responsibilities, since a testimony of faith and an ecclesial relationship to both the local diocese in which the school is situated and the broader Catholic community are essential to a Catholic school's existence and should be a point of great pride. It is an identity to celebrate and cherish.

Effective leaders also must intentionally commit to a

18   *Chapter 1*

community-based, collaborative process when revising the mission statement, which usually is coordinated by a central mission committee. When constituting this committee (or any other), it is important to select a small but representative group of members. A small committee (no more than ten members, plus the president, who serves as chair) is efficient, flexible, and easy to convene, given the myriad responsibilities of today's educators.

Too often leaders assemble large, unwieldy committees in an attempt to be inclusive. While inclusivity is critical to the process, inclusivity can be upheld in multiple ways: through focus groups, e-surveys, and town hall meetings, all of which reflect a community-based, collaborative model.[14] A large committee risks getting bogged down to the point where the revision of the mission statement takes excessive time and energy. The president, who has ultimate responsibility for successfully completing this task, needs to set the project's pace by developing a tight time frame to accomplish the work (no more than six months) while maintaining broad consultation. In other words, the process is intense because it calls for the hard work of carefully distilling words and ideas, all of which takes discipline and focus.

Too many schools embrace lengthy mission statements that reflect the dedicated work of mission committee members who pored over their tasks for many months and used an ongoing consultative method for community input. The leader overseeing this process must challenge the mission committee and the community to realize that "less is more." A tightly written mission statement packs more inspirational power than a wordy document with multiple paragraphs that attempts to be all things to all people.

Should the academic community seek to elaborate on the mission statement, it can simultaneously develop a complementary document that addresses the hallmarks or central characteristics of the school's history, traditions, values, and contributions. This more detailed document then serves as a

The Centrality of the Mission 19

companion piece to the mission statement, and both statements should be promulgated in all communications.

When a school revises its mission statement, the president has the critical responsibility to involve the board of trustees in the process, as this body is the ultimate authority that approves or rejects the final recommendation. Some boards may want to be heavily involved in the rewriting process itself; others may want to see draft versions as the process progresses. Although not recommended, a few boards may decide to become involved only when they have received the president's final recommendation, offered in the name of the school community. There are many reasons why this last model is problematic, as there is always the potential that the board will reject the recommendation, a decision that results in a demoralizing experience for the entire community after months of work. To avoid this situation, it is advisable to involve the board throughout the process so that trustees are not caught off guard by the final recommendation or placed in the difficult position of rejecting a proposal that is new to them. Regardless of the level of engagement, board involvement is critical in the process, as it has the final authority to approve or reject the final recommendation.

This collaborative process of revising the mission statement can be very rewarding, as there is great satisfaction and ownership when the entire community sees this project completed in a timely and successful way. A Catholic school should celebrate this new way of articulating its mission by promoting the revised mission statement internally and externally and incorporating the new mission statement throughout the life and fabric of the community.

This process of revising a mission statement is described at some length because it can serve as a model for high-impact leadership at its very best. Presidents are frequently tasked with the need for school-wide consultation on several serious issues such as strategic planning, campus master planning, and accreditation reports/visits, all of which also involve important engagement with the board of trustees. While departments and

20   *Chapter 1*

other smaller academic units have their methods of securing input from colleagues, a president is rightfully expected to involve the entire community in significant areas that impact the overall well-being and reputation of the school. To summarize this recommended process for making substantive change through high-impact leadership:

1. Commit publicly to a collaborative, consultative model of leadership that includes all school constituencies—a process that is "by the community, for the community, and with the community."

2. Articulate to the community the "why," "why now," and "how" concerning the project as a whole before starting a community-based consultative process; keep the process itself as simple as possible.

3. Appoint a planning committee that is representative of various school constituencies but few in number to allow nimbleness, flexibility, and the ability to schedule both regular and ad hoc meetings as needed.

4. Provide the school community with various means for submitting their opinions and feedback, including town hall meetings, focus groups, e-surveys, and other effective means of consultation.

5. Adhere to rigorous "best practice" standards of assessing feedback in order to secure accurate data and ensure a systematic way to collect community feedback.

6. Plan and promote all committee meetings carefully, and send relevant materials and notice of the meetings well in advance in order to maximize the participants' preparation. Doing this signals the meeting's importance and the seriousness with which the input will be treated.

7. Keep the committee meetings focused, with sufficient time for preliminary group feedback at the end.

8. Listen carefully. Leaders must refrain from using any session as an opportunity to update the school community on a range of issues (enrollment, fundraising, alumni activities, etc.).

9. Set a tight time frame for the entire process. If executed well, a school-wide planning process should take approximately six months in order to maintain focus and genuine energy for the project. Community morale will be adversely impacted if the process is prolonged or unwieldy.

10. Update the board of trustees regularly throughout the process and invite the board's participation as desired or necessary.

Conclusion

The centrality of a school's mission statement cannot be overstated, as it both animates and motivates the school community daily. However, the mission statement also speaks to the integrity of the school itself, as demonstrated by its role in the accreditation process. As the Association of Governing Boards of Universities and Colleges (AGB) notes: "Not surprisingly, a first task for an accreditation visiting team is usually to review the current mission statement. As the visit develops, the team appraises the statement's congruence with institutional objectives, programs, services, and resources."[15] Whether during an accreditation visit or more typically in the day-to-day life of the school, a Catholic community is responsible for promoting its mission as the core of its identity, as it contributes to the Church's centuries-old commitment to explore truth in the context of faith.

The Role of the President and the Centrality of the Mission

- Understand the importance of education as an ecclesial mission within the Catholic Church.
- Appreciate the Catholic intellectual tradition.
- Know the school's legacy—its founding, its history, and its contribution to the Church.
- Never hesitate to promote the school's mission.

22 *Chapter 1*

- Support all pastoral dimensions of the Office of Mission/Campus Ministry.
- Respect the unique role of the Theology/Religious Studies Department.
- Provide the faculty and staff with ample mission-related professional development opportunities.
- Assure frequent availability of Eucharistic celebrations, retreats, and service opportunities for all members of the school community, especially students.
- Commit to assessing mission effectiveness.
- Use the mission statement revision process as a model for intentional collaboration.

Key Questions

1. Does your school have a clearly articulated, faith-based mission statement?

2. How does this stated mission impact the daily life of your school community? Cite specific rituals, celebrations, and opportunities.

3. How do teachers integrate the school's mission in their classes? Cite examples.

4. How does the staff incorporate the mission into their daily work and office activities? Cite examples.

5. How do students demonstrate mission awareness? Cite examples.

6. How does your school measure the varied ways the community embraces the mission?

7. Is the mission statement prominent in the school's communications?

8. Do you, as the school leader, incorporate the mission into all opportunities when addressing the varied constituents of the community?

9. Does the mission statement need revision? What process will accomplish this goal in a consultative, collaborative manner? When and how will the board of trustees be involved?

The Centrality of the Mission   23

10. How will the revised mission statement be appropriately promulgated and celebrated?

Case Study: The Centrality of the Mission

The archdiocese hires you to transform Saint A's High School, whose Catholic mission and identity have waned dramatically over the years, despite the school's eighty-two-year history and long tradition of strong academic performance. Saint A's academic record continues to distinguish the school.

Situated in an urban environment, most of Saint A's students are not of the Catholic faith. In addition, the majority of the faculty and staff are not Catholic. The Eucharist is rarely celebrated and few specific Christian symbols can be seen around campus. Student retreats have not been held for several years; Advent and Lenten liturgical celebrations rarely take place. Although religion classes are listed in accordance with the archdiocesan curricular requirements, the actual curricula and pedagogy stress world religions, with a heavy emphasis on "what Catholicism is not" rather than "what Catholicism is."

Financially the school is stable, as many families utilize the state's school voucher program to attend Saint A's, making Catholic education accessible to many families who otherwise would not attend. The school has a very small endowment and its cash reserves are modest. There is no organized fundraising history to speak of, although facilities have been adequately maintained and administrative and academic technologies have recently been upgraded due to a major grant from a local foundation. The school has no formally established board of trustees.

The situation you encounter at Saint A's troubles you greatly, as the school significantly differs from your experience of "living the mission" within a Catholic school. How do you reverse the situation? How do you plan to interact with the archdiocese concerning the situation? What immediate steps should you take? What type of planning will be effective in this situation? What goals should immediately be established as top priorities?

24   *Chapter 1*

Equally important, How will you work with the students, the faculty, and the staff? How will you manage new enrollment strategies and hiring practices? How will you strengthen and continue the school's robust academic reputation?

The archdiocese has given you three years to transform the situation at Saint A's. Is this time frame realistic? Do you have the appropriate personnel and necessary financial resources to realize the archdiocesan three-year goal? If not, how will the needed resources be secured or how will you explain your suggested adjustments to the goal?

Notes

1. "Catholic Education on the Margins."
2. The bylaws of most Catholic schools require the president to be a practicing Catholic.
3. Pope John Paul II, *Apostolic Constitution,* 1.
4. Dwyer, *New Dictionary of Catholic Social Thought.*
5. Pope John Paul II, *Apostolic Constitution,* 39.
6. Nicolás, "Depth, Universality, and Learned Ministry," 2.
7. Pope John Paul II, *Apostolic Constitution,* 23; Vatican Council II, Gaudium et Spes, 59.
8. Pope Francis, "Audience with the Delegation."
9. Vatican Council II, Gaudium et Spes, 1.
10. Pope Francis, *Laudato Si'.*
11. Groome, *What Makes Education Catholic.*
12. Holtschneider, "Treasure in Earthen Vessels," 20–34; Cunningham, "On Teaching Theology."
13. The exception is the extremely rare occasion when the board of trustees votes—after extensive deliberation—to change the mission of the institution.
14. In all instances the process must use highly reliable research methods to ensure accurate assessment of community input and feedback. See Hayes and Ruschman, "Marketing Research," 35–38.
15. AGB, *Higher Education Governing Boards,* 2.

2

The Strategic Plan as Institutional Road Map

A CENTRAL ELEMENT TO THE SUCCESS of a president's tenure is the ability to oversee the organization's comprehensive strategic planning process, including the strategic plan's clear articulation and implementation upon formal approval by the board of trustees. The importance of this responsibility cannot be overstated, as strategic plans inspire and motivate the entire community through rigorous analysis of the present in order to shape a solid, financially secure future. Regardless of the size of the institution, a strong strategic plan can transform a school. These simple, straightforward words are true but belie the amount of thinking, research, organization, and consultation that comprise a process that yields a truly transformational document. It is critical, therefore, that presidents and other senior administrators demonstrate unwavering belief in the necessity, relevance, and potential impact of the entire undertaking, as hard work, significant time, and a great expenditure of energy are involved.

Opportunities and Challenges in the Strategic Planning Process

Throughout the strategic planning process, the president often faces a variety of challenges. However, every challenge brings

26 Chapter 2

an opportunity to exercise high-impact leadership, as evidenced when a president exercises these key qualities throughout a strategic planning process:

1. The president clearly connects the process to the Catholic school's mission by continually emphasizing the mission's foundational nature and its North Star role in all school undertakings. In planning documents and in all representations to the community, high-impact leadership reiterates the enduring and central role of the mission, even while pointing the community to its future realization. Given this centrality of mission, however, the strategic planning process is usually not the time to attempt a major revision of the institution's mission statement, as the community can easily get buried in this revision process and the actual strategic planning opportunity can be lost or extensively delayed. Ideally the revision of the mission statement, if needed, is undertaken outside the cycle of strategic planning.

2. The president develops a future-oriented plan from the beginning. Here is the opportunity for the school to see itself in a new way, to reimagine itself at new levels of quality, innovation, and overall excellence. Where does this school see itself in the future? Specifically, where does the school see itself in the next five years? Too often strategic plans miss this significant opportunity by merely rearticulating the status quo: "This is the way we do things." Many people do not like risk and fear an unknown future. Organizations can become complacent, and leaders may often hear, "It's already working; why change it?" It is undoubtedly more comfortable to repeat "what is" than to explore, in a rigorous fashion, "what could be." While there will always be skeptics who question the reason for "yet another" strategic plan, the president has the responsibility to present this process as an opportunity rather than an insurmountable challenge, with the aim of convincing the majority of the community that "no school stands still." With trust, mutual support, and high

The Strategic Plan as Institutional Road Map 27

levels of collaboration, a community can shape a stronger future for itself, even if on a modest scale.

3. A successful president aims high, that is, develops a truly *strategic* plan. Strategic planning often requires making difficult, uncomfortable decisions and it is therefore a "disruptive experience" in that sense. This is the moment to frame central issues and ask key questions. Examples of such important queries might include the following: What goals will bring our school to a higher level of excellence? Should some academic programs or departments be eliminated while new programs are added? Will such restructuring lead to increased efficiency and better communication? Is this the time to grow enrollment? Should the school build a new facility on its campus? Are the current information resources and technologies seamless, efficient, and user-friendly, or is a major migration to a more robust system necessary? These are the types of strategic questions that move away from the easier query: What goals fit our current operating budget and capital budget? While there are many implications for strategic goals that impact the budget, infrastructure, personnel, and many other areas, the leader must set the bar high to keep strategic planning truly strategic. For this reason, the process needs to stay at the 40,000-foot level.

However, a word of caution is in order. While every strategic plan should have stretch goals, all stretch goals must be within the realm of possibility and genuinely attainable. The creative process should be rooted in reality but envisioned in new ways; it should not be a fantasy, devoid of a grounding in the real world. Naive, wishful thinking weakens the credibility of the entire project, impacts morale, and sets the school up for failure. High-impact leaders take calculated risks, but they are not reckless. For this reason the president must have the courage, knowledge, and deep experience needed to guide the school through this process and the development of the sustainable financial model required to support it.

28   *Chapter 2*

This point in the planning process is the true test of genuine leadership, as the president must guide the community (including the board) to distill and embrace only those significant goals that stretch the community but do not break it. This is the moment in the process where leaders, trusting in their own expertise and experience, have the opportunity to exercise real vision and do so with confidence and purpose—weighing a delicate balance that, if lost, is difficult to regain.

4. High-impact leadership also develops a method for achieving the tactical issues (the 20,000-foot level) that inevitably arise during a strategic planning process. Questions that are exceptionally important in realizing the overall success of the school's strategic plan identify the "who" (specific person or department responsible for a goal), the "when" (specific date for completion of a goal), the "how" (specific steps to accomplish a goal), the "how much" (budget required to accomplish a goal), and the "how to evaluate" (specific assessment tools to measure goal success or failure). To address these issues concerning the actual implementation of the plan, senior administrators should simultaneously develop a second parallel implementation document that captures all relevant tactical questions that emerge throughout the strategic planning process. Structured like the strategic plan itself (for example, mirroring its major categories), this implementation document is the tactical engine that drives achievement of the strategic goals; it is a working document that will evolve through numerous updates. The president, however, must ensure that the senior leadership team does not become so focused on developing this implementation document that actual strategic-level planning is unnecessarily delayed.

5. The president understands that there is neither a perfect strategic plan nor a perfect strategic planning process. Every leader in a Catholic school community must select a process that fits its specific culture, with the understanding that the

The Strategic Plan as Institutional Road Map 29

selected process directly impacts the overall strength of the final document.

6. The president makes sure all constituencies (students and parents, faculty, staff, trustees, alumni) have a voice in the process, including the opportunity to participate in some meaningful way, although the methods for inclusion may vary for different groups (town hall meetings, focus groups, e-surveys, to cite a few examples). As noted in chapter 1, such sessions promote an open exchange of ideas; they also demonstrate the president's confidence and trust in all members of the school community. This inclusive, collaborative process is essential and is the only way by which the community will truly own the results of the planning process. Community investment in the plan's realization and a certain pride in helping to achieve its success will result from a strategic planning process that is "by the community, for the community, and with the community," that is, an inclusive and transparent process that has integrity and ensures credibility.

A central, small committee (no more than ten members) is needed to organize, coordinate, and guide this strategic planning collaborative process, with the president serving as the chair. Every major area of the school (admissions, academics, development, facilities, finance, information resources/technologies, marketing/communications, and student life) should have a seat on this committee, as strategic goals inevitably intersect with all areas of the school and ultimately shape a matrix of fresh ideas. Within this representative committee, the president needs to foster genuine openness and debate to demonstrate confidence in the planning committee and respect for the expertise and experience of all committee members—a model of trust and a level of discourse that sets the tone for school-wide consultation.

This school-wide, community-based strategic planning process, however, should not result in a document that is a "wish

30 *Chapter 2*

list" from everyone in the organization, nor should it be a compilation of everyone's priorities. An effective leader must guard against any tendency to "be all things to all people." To attempt too much or to lose focus invariably weakens the school, the realization of its mission, and its overall achievement of excellence and ultimate success. The strategic planning process is not an opportunity to simply add programs, departments, or personnel, with no apparent limit. A strong strategic plan trims and eliminates weak or outdated processes and programs, even as it may add new processes or programs. The emphasis must be on quality, not quantity.

This temptation to be "all things to all people" is one reason strategic planning is hard work. A certain nostalgia for long-standing programs and ways of doing things can grip certain members of a school and then spread throughout the community. The president must navigate these waters with care, understanding, and respect—but also demonstrate the necessity and enduring benefit of making tough decisions throughout the strategic planning process.

7. To prevent this all-things-to-all-people approach, the planning process is lean, focused, and carefully structured in order to yield a few carefully distilled strategic goals for each major area of the school.[1] A high-impact president promotes an overarching plan that reflects a clear, streamlined model that is concise and comprehensive.

8. Successful presidents actively resist the temptation to project too far into the future. For this reason, a fresh strategic planning process conducted every five years is the ideal cycle. This allows time for the realization of significant goals that complement formal accreditation cycles. In addition, a five-year plan does not risk the possibility that strategic plans are based on too many unknown economic and demographic factors.

9. The president sets a predetermined amount of time (no more than six to eight months) to complete school-wide consultation,

The Strategic Plan as Institutional Road Map 31

research, writing (of course, there will be multiple drafts), and formal board approval. This model of planning, however, makes three key assumptions: (a) that the school has a thorough understanding of recommendations from external reviewers, such as accrediting agencies and audit firms; (b) that the school promotes a culture that values the importance of accurate data and its proper use;[2] (c) that the school practices ongoing assessment in multiple areas, such as enrollment patterns or the effectiveness of enterprise information systems, to mention three critical components of any organization. To embark on strategic planning within an already established "best practice" culture tightens the process and allotted time frame, resulting in an intense but overall successful experience for the community. It also prevents waning community interest and energy should the planning process extend over a too-long period of time.

10. High-impact leadership keeps the process simple. However, this does not mean the process is easy or simplistic. On the contrary, the president must embrace a highly rigorous methodology that presses the community to seek sustainable solutions versus the superficial "quick fix." Moreover, the president should be expected to have a thorough knowledge of best practices and solid data-informed recommendations when shaping strategic goals, especially in the wake of the intense COVID-19 years. Topics such as an assessment of new levels of parental engagement, post-pandemic applications of technology, shifts in enrollment, and other revenue sources—all merit inclusion in the type of thorough analysis that contributes to successful strategic planning.[3]

One component of this required analytical rigor centers on developing benchmarks based on a carefully researched list of aspirant schools. These schools are comparable but also regarded as "thought leaders" in the educational field; they outrank one's own school in either international, national, state, or regional standings.[4] For example, an all-girls' independent school should benchmark against other all-girls' independent schools. Using

32   *Chapter 2*

standard key performance indicators (e.g., percentage of faculty with advanced degrees, faculty-to-student ratio, total enrollment, international programs offered), this task helps a school identify its "gaps" or weaknesses but also identify and affirm its strengths. At the same time, developing a "peer school" list using the same key performance indicators assists in identifying the immediate "competition," that is, the peer schools whose impact a president should never underestimate. A careful, thorough analysis of this comparative data from aspirant and peer institutions will assist a president when attempting to formulate strategic plans around best practice principles. An added benefit is that this research will often highlight those programs within one's own school that provide distinguishing value-added features to celebrate.

Essential Content

While each Catholic school must focus on topics that are relevant to its specific context, five content areas are essential when developing a document that ensures institutional vitality: (1) the opportunity to enhance mission effectiveness throughout the community; (2) an accurate assessment of current general opportunities and threats to Catholic education; (3) specific demographic analysis and projected impact on enrollment; (4) a financial model that will support all goals of the plan; and (5) the development of a campus master plan. These five interrelated areas of a school's strategic plan provide the essential framework for all detailed school-wide and departmental planning and are crucial for realizing the significant opportunities that strategic planning presents to the academic community.

Mission

Enhancing mission effectiveness is an indispensable component of strategic planning in the context of a Catholic school. How do specific strategic goals fortify mission effectiveness? Does the

The Strategic Plan as Institutional Road Map   33

school require an Office of Mission Effectiveness? Should campus ministry increase service opportunities? Is there attractive space for worship on campus? Does the school offer sufficient, mission-related, substantive professional development opportunities for faculty and staff? Should service-learning opportunities expand to regional, national, or international sites as part of the larger strategic goal to have students experience more diversity and develop cross-cultural awareness and sensitivity? These and many other mission-related questions should be asked when engaged in strategic planning.

Current Challenges

To address certain areas of concern within higher education, economist Quentin Wodon cites a recent report to the International Federation of Catholic Universities (IFCU) in which Corinne Mellul summarizes the post–COVID-19 pressures affecting universities today: (a) financial constraints; (b) reductions in international student mobility; (c) the impact of technology; (d) the rise of micro-credentials as potential alternatives to traditional degrees; all of which lead to (e) broader debates about the future of higher education.[5] To this sobering list Wodon adds that high-income countries also experience (f) a demographic shift due to lower fertility rates and (g) a movement toward secularization/pluralism regarding faith.[6] While not all topics on this list impact every K-12 school or higher education institution, most do.

Demographics

When addressing the broad areas identified by Mellul and Wodon, the school must analyze its current demographic situation vis-à-vis specific regional, state, national, and international demographic trends that may directly impact a specific setting. In addition, a school's internal data concerning enrollment, retention, graduation rates, and other significant key performance

34   *Chapter 2*

indicators comprise a second layer of information; while a third layer of inspection often sorts individual cohorts (e.g., by grade level, country of origin, and other categories).

The seriousness of the demographic situation cannot be understated, as Nathan D. Grawe notes when addressing the current situation in higher education:

> As demographic forces promise to reshape the size and composition of future cohorts of college-going students, many institutions recognize the need to take proactive measures that ensure their sustainability and effectiveness for the future. Of course, institutions are perpetually evolving. What makes the current demographic challenge a bit different is its magnitude. From a peak just prior to the financial crisis in 2008 through 2017, the number of babies born in the United States fell by more than 500,000 (Centers for Disease Control and Prevention, 2013, 2019). At the same time, migration and fertility patterns continue to remake the population, producing declining shares of non-Hispanic whites and residences of the Northeast—that is, moving away from populations that have disproportionately attended colleges in the past. As if concerns about the domestic market for higher education were not enough, we have also witnessed a recent decline in new international student enrollments (Institute of International Education, 2019).[7]

Of course, shifting demographics also seriously impact K-12 schools. Educators look to ongoing studies conducted by the National Center for Education Statistics (NCES).[8] The NCEA also provides excellent data that tracks relevant demographic and enrollment trends in Catholic K-12 schools and continually offers clear snapshots of current data, such as total national enrollments, percentages concerning student diversity, and full-time equivalent professional staffing numbers, to cite a few of the areas that the association regularly monitors.[9]

Strategic planning must engage this type of essential information by asking tough questions: Do these current data points

The Strategic Plan as Institutional Road Map 35

and projections constitute genuine threats to the success of the school? If so, how? Do these current data points and projections provide opportunities? How do they influence a campus master plan? Do the trustees appreciate the significance of these trends? Will this data prompt the school to consider new organizational structures?

Financial Analysis

Using accurate data and enrollment analysis assures a solid foundation for financial planning, in addition to the many other factors required to secure a clear financial picture of a school: current discount rate, financial aid allocations, tuition projections, amount of permanent debt, debt capacity, projected costs to address deferred maintenance issues, projected overall operating budget, current restricted and unrestricted endowment, current investment portfolio profile, average annual fund giving, and projected employee compensation, to cite some of the many areas that warrant intense financial analysis.

In this exercise of genuine stewardship and fiduciary responsibility, presidents and boards address an abundance of financial questions on a regular basis, assuring the type of operational vitality that the NCEA identifies in its *National Standards and Benchmarks for Effective Catholic Elementary and Secondary Schools*.[10] Strong financial vigilance is magnified during strategic planning: Does the school engage in multiyear financial planning? Do tuition rates assure a long-standing commitment within Catholic education to access and affordability? Is the discounted rate too high and used merely to "fill seats," with the serious effect of generating significantly decreased net tuition revenue per student? Does the school's overall net tuition revenue cover operational expenses? Should the school attempt to close the gap between the net tuition revenues and the actual operating expenses?[11] Does the budget cover both short-term expenses and long-term strategies? Is there an adequate cash reserve available in case of an emergency? What key points of

36   Chapter 2

information do recent external financial audits provide? Do the finances provide strict adherence to a labor/management agreement (applicable in only certain schools)? Can some departments restructure in order to be more efficient and effective? Which academic programs are highly successful, and which programs may need to be eliminated? This last calculation cannot be made solely on class enrollment numbers, as enrollment may be low in some disciplines but enhance the overall academic experience for students. For example, the study of Latin provides a solid liberal arts experience but may garner low to modest enrollments. When posing this program elimination question, therefore, many factors need to enter the calculation, including student evaluations and external standardized test results. A carefully managed budget, however, cannot usually sustain every class that faculty members wish to offer.

Minimally, the strategic plan (and especially its parallel implementation/tactical document) must protect the school's financial health by incorporating the following:

- A balanced operating budget. (Tactic: Monitor departmental spending throughout the fiscal year and immediately raise "red flags" when certain departments exceed spending ahead of schedule. For example, 75 percent of budget spent when only halfway through the fiscal year.) As Melody Rose and Larry D. Large note in their work *Higher Education Business Models Under Stress: Achieving Graceful Transitions in the Academy,* "campus leaders should make maintaining a balanced budget over multiple fiscal periods their operational North Star. The increase in campus bankruptcies and closures demonstrates what happens when an institution's budget enters a dreaded cycle of unsustainable deficits."[12]
- A strategy to pay off existing debt. (Tactic: Allocate a certain percentage of the annual operating budget to debt repayment.)

The Strategic Plan as Institutional Road Map 37

- A strategy to increase the endowment each year, even if only modestly.
- A policy that periodically evaluates investment managers. (Tactic: Evaluate contracts and obtain several competing requests for proposals at least once every three years.)
- A policy that seeks highly regarded financial auditing firms. (Tactic: Evaluate contracts and obtain several competing requests for proposals at least once every three years.)
- Planned cycles for basic facility maintenance and campus upkeep.
- Planned cycles for technology maintenance, renewal of leases, and hardware and software purchases.

These strategic goals and their counterpart tactical directives (and many other operational matters related to the use of school-issued credit cards, limited authorization to sign contracts, adherence to financial deadlines, and so forth) are critical to leading a successful school.

These broad factors—demographic trends, specific school-based enrollment data, and comprehensive financial analysis—will have a significant impact on planning, with the result that may lead to strategic decisions that eliminate extraneous academic programs, departments, or positions while fortifying and possibly adding certain programs and departments that reflect mission-criticality, efficiency, effectiveness, and ability to meet the emerging needs of students. For example, decisions concerning technology upgrades or building projects may need to be accelerated or delayed. Cocurricular offerings may need to be expanded or restructured. Offerings in the athletics program may need to be reinvigorated or eliminated. Presidents cannot flinch in the face of these major decisions, all embedded within a rigorous strategic planning process.

When significant (often interrelated) red flags arise throughout the school's enrollment and financial profile, including significant deferred maintenance, low enrollments (with each

38   *Chapter 2*

school needing to determine what constitutes a financially sustainable enrollment), insufficient net tuition revenue to meet operating needs, weak endowment (vis-à-vis the operating budget), and significant debt, the president must be prepared to take some perhaps painful recommendations to the board of trustees, namely, that it may be in the school's best interest to explore alternative educational models in collaboration with another institution, including consolidation, partnership, affiliation, or merger.[13] While all Catholic schools can seek alliances within the broader community, Catholic colleges and universities might also explore strategic corporate alliances, although this may require a reconsideration of academic structures, a revision of the curriculum, and a careful consideration of alignment with Catholic values. Paul LeBlanc and Kristine Clerkin note the benefits of competency-based education:

> Competency-based education (CBE) provides an opportunity to close the gap through partnerships between institutions and employers because it gives both parties a shared vocabulary to talk about the challenge. Employers do not think about curriculum and courses—they think about what people can do in terms of their competencies. CBE programs do the same, shifting from what students know to what students can do with what they know. Moreover, because CBE starts with clarity around those competencies, it forces education providers to look hard at what employers need to make sure the competencies are the right ones that will lead to job orders and workplace success and can be defended.[14]

Although time-consuming and expensive to run, every alternative educational model may yield an enhanced quality of student life and strengthened academic reputation, improved operational efficiency, increased assets, a more robust marketing position, and many other advantages not realized by many autonomous but struggling Catholic schools.[15]

In some cases a school may find that the strategic planning

The Strategic Plan as Institutional Road Map   39

process underscores the need to close entirely—after multiple failed attempts to make ends meet have only resulted in extraordinary stress on the institution and a demoralized community.[16] In these situations, presidents must help their communities face the harsh reality with transparency, strength, grace, and dignity, marking the moment as the fulfillment of an important, critical mission with a legacy that now lives among its graduates and all who served the institution.

Campus Master Planning

The final essential component of any strategic planning process includes the development of a campus facilities master plan or a significant update to an existing plan. Regardless of the school size (large or small) or location (urban, suburban, or rural), a campus master plan is an indispensable tool, as the campus "never gets a second chance to make a first impression."[17] This component of planning examines the campus as a whole and includes multiple variables: safety issues, enrollments (current and projected), vehicle and pedestrian traffic, landscaping, lighting, and the number of current (and projected) buildings and classrooms, to cite a few examples.

A facilities master plan ensures better overall planning for enrollment and finances and enables a board or president to make sound financial choices. Assuming that there are no safety issues at stake, campus master planning will typically generate multiple questions: Do we repair the infrastructure of a building that is scheduled to be demolished in three years? Are existing classrooms sufficiently flexible to support contemporary teaching and learning methods (such as technology enhanced active learning [TEAL]), or should the school renovate or build new facilities? Like so many aspects of strategic planning, facilities planning is both science and art, and the process of strategic thinking provides the opportunity to reimagine the physical aspect of a campus, even within limited space. Once a school commits to this important dimension of its strategic plan—a step

40   *Chapter 2*

that often includes hiring architectural firms that specialize in this type of educational planning—more tactical choices, such as time line, appear in the implementation document.[18]

Promulgation

Once finally approved by the board of trustees, the new strategic plan needs to be widely promulgated throughout the community, and there are at least three different formats to use in achieving this important step:

1. Develop a brief executive summary booklet that contains the mission statement, an opening joint letter from the board chair and president, a list of the current trustees, and all major categories of the strategic plan: academics, development, enrollment, facilities, finance, information resources, technology, marketing and communications, and student life. Within each of these planning categories, provide bullet point summaries of the identified goals. An attractive executive summary booklet is a marketing piece that promotes the school's overall excellence and often presents photographs of students, faculty, and staff interacting in curricular or cocurricular activities in order to personalize the plan.[19] This executive summary should be widely distributed, and the offices of the president, admissions, alumni, communications, and development, among others, should act as central distribution points for the many constituents whom the school serves. Rapidly deployed, an executive summary is a highly effective snapshot of the strategic plan and should be posted on the school's website, with hard copies readily available to the general school community throughout the five-year planning cycle.

2. Develop a detailed but brief comprehensive strategic planning document—with goals, a listing of departments that are accountable for implementation, and key dates for goal fulfillment—and make it easily available to all stakeholders.

The Strategic Plan as Institutional Road Map   41

3. Develop a highly detailed implementation document, published at the same time, that is primarily intended for internal use by trustees and senior administrators. This comprehensive tactical document, developed in parallel with a strategic plan, states all the steps necessary to achieve the various goals (who, when, how, how much [money], and how to [evaluate]) and serves as the genuine engine for the strategic plan's implementation. It is indispensable in realizing a successful strategic plan.

Implementation

After the conclusion of every fiscal year (usually June 30), the president should submit to the full board an executive summary that outlines progress on fulfilling all strategic goals. If there has been a significant delay in achieving a goal within its designated time period, reasons for this delay should be clearly stated and in some cases certain adjustments to specific sections within the implementation document may be necessary. This report to the board should also be made available to senior administrators; it should include overall budget allocations, financial expenditures on the goals to date, and initial results from measuring goal effectiveness. This report also holds the board, the president, and all senior administrators highly accountable and may be used in accreditation reviews, financial audits, and other external evaluations that examine a school's integrity and financial stability—an achievement worthy of the many intense hours of collaborative work.

Conclusion

Developing and implementing a successful strategic plan requires discipline, focus, and sophistication. It often tests a president's leadership qualities and skills and measures a president's ability to organize, motivate, inspire, distill, prioritize, and communicate effectively. For this reason Adam Bryant and Kevin Sharer address the important skill of simplifying the complexity

42 *Chapter 2*

of planning in their work *The CEO Test: Master the Challenges that Make or Break All Leaders.* They note the following:

> The core skill of simplifying complexity . . . is an essential tool for navigating and wringing insights from the onslaught of information and infinite choices that leaders face. . . . This ability to simplify complexity is a necessary time-management tool . . . that will make you more effective and more efficient by quickly bringing clarity to complex subjects that are fraught with ambiguity and risk, and will help you bring people along with crystal-clear communications about various challenges and the strategies for tackling them. The skill of simplifying complexity is not widely shared, and leaders need to make a conscious effort to practice it themselves. . . . A critical test of this skill for leaders is whether they can use it to articulate a clear, galvanizing plan for what the company is trying to achieve. Can they stand up in front of their employees and, in a simple and memorable way, explain where the company is headed and why, along with a plan, timetable, and ways to measure progress along the route? This is the cornerstone of any organization.[20]

Bryant and Sharer make a key point: the president has the responsibility to present strategic goals clearly and meaningfully to the broader academic community, even while relying on highly qualified staff to conduct enrollment and financial analysis and other valuable studies that provide essential components of a strategic plan.[21] It is also the president who must engage the board of trustees throughout the process, as the board ultimately approves the plan (a topic discussed in chapter 5, on governance).

When done well, the strategic plan brings confidence and direction to the community and a renewed commitment to its mission and legacy. It assures parents and alumni that the school has a solid future, helps attract new students, enhances the quality of the student experience, brings fitting recognition to faculty and staff, sparks the interest of donors, and demonstrates intentional fulfillment of accreditation requirements.

High-Impact Leaders and the Strategic Plan as Institutional Road Map

- Understand the importance of grounding the strategic plan in the school's mission.
- Appreciate the multiple opportunities and challenges within a strategic planning process.
- Structure the collaborative process in a way that maximizes community input but also keeps the process going at a brisk pace.
- Assure all students of their important role in the strategic planning process.
- Solicit and rely on the creative input of faculty, administrators, staff, students, parents, alumni, and trustees.
- Commit to extensive demographic analysis as an essential content component.
- Appreciate the identified aspirant schools and the impact of peer competitors.
- Know the school's current financial situation and projections thoroughly; understand this area as an essential content component.
- Use a campus master plan to guide all facility and technology investments.
- Promulgate the completed plan in multiple ways to different constituencies.
- Secure trustee authorization, commitment, and participation throughout the process.

Key Questions

1. Have you ever held a senior leadership role in a strategic planning process?

2. If yes, what keywords would you use to describe this experience?

3. Have you directly experienced campus master planning? Did this effort include collaboration with architects, engineers, contractors, and others?

44   *Chapter 2*

4. How would you prepare a board of trustees and school community to undertake a strategic planning process?

5. What specific steps would you take to ensure a collaborative process within a concise time frame, one that is genuinely strategic?

6. Has your school identified aspirant and peer schools for purposes of comprehensive planning?

7. Have you ever developed a sustainable financial model? What are the key components of the model?

8. What value-added features characterize your school? Are certain areas in need of immediate improvement?

9. Have you ever been forced to eliminate a curricular or cocurricular program? Describe the experience.

10. Are there financial red flags at your school? How do you plan to address them?

Case Study: Strategic Planning

You have just arrived at your school as the new president, and one of your top priorities is to develop a fresh five-year strategic plan. During your hiring process the trustees were pleased to see that you bring experience in this area, as they saw a genuine need for this type of strategic process at their school, especially related to new facilities.

You announce to the school that you are prepared to lead the community in a collaborative strategic planning process that will last approximately six months. You indicate that while all aspects of school life will be examined, the most pressing need is in the area of facilities, as a recent accreditation report noted the lack of physical space on campus (both academic and social), given the school's enrollment. The board has already committed to raising the money for one new capital project over the next five years.

After consulting with your senior administrative team you appoint a representative coordinating committee to oversee the planning process, a committee that you will chair. You have

The Strategic Plan as Institutional Road Map   45

already started to gather key documents that are critical to this process, including the most recent accreditation report, studies concerning enrollment projections, the data that was used to shape the current campus master plan, and a recent external assessment of the school's administrative and academic technology needs.

You embark on the process at the beginning of October after scheduling weekly meetings with the small coordinating committee that you have assembled. By mid-October this committee has posted a complete schedule for community consultations, with an array of opportunities and formats for contributing, including e-surveys, focus groups, and open meetings. The board has chosen to use its trustee committee structure to engage at this stage of the process. By November the school is thoroughly immersed in the strategic planning process, even as the regularly scheduled classes and cocurricular activities go forward as usual.

As the coordinating committee begins to assess the strategic goals identified by the trustees, it becomes clear that a new athletic complex is its top priority for the next major building project on campus, even though an adequate athletic facility already exists. The board has already identified several key donors eager to support construction of this state-of-the-art facility, including new exercise machines equipped with biofeedback software, film and meeting rooms, and a small food court. Many trustees are former athletes themselves who now have sons, granddaughters, and other relatives who play on the school's various teams. They also see that a new complex has the potential to recruit new student-athletes. It is clear that enthusiastic support for this capital project exists among the trustees.

When you and the coordinating committee assess the wider community feedback, however, there is a strong preference among faculty for a new learning commons, as the current library is small, dark, and extraordinarily difficult to navigate, especially since the building has been repeatedly modified over the years and has unreliable internet connectivity. There is also an insufficient number of classrooms on campus and the

46 Chapter 2

academic technology is outdated. The faculty envision a state-of-the-art digital commons; it would be a campus hub with TEAL classrooms and space for directors who oversee information resources and technologies, including online offerings. In addition, the learning commons would provide rooms for tutoring and small group collaboration sessions, several faculty offices, space dedicated to meetings and social activities, and an attractive bistro. This commons will also model the school's standards for future upgrades to existing campus classrooms as well as impact the ongoing development of online programs.

As the emerging facility priorities within the strategic planning process are made known to the wider community in December, it becomes clear that the board and the faculty are extremely divided in their priorities. The board cites strong donor interest, including for a prominent "naming opportunity." The planning e-survey results also indicate strong alumni support for a new athletic complex. Conversely, the faculty claims that "sports get all the attention" at the school and that it is time to prioritize academic needs. The faculty are upset that "donors are controlling the school" and now demand more faculty representation on the steering committee.

How do you address this situation? What advice do you give to the coordinating committee concerning how to proceed? How will you work with your board of trustees and faculty in the months ahead? Should you add more faculty representatives to the strategic steering committee, as requested? What do the students think? Can you complete this strategic planning process in the projected six-month time frame? Do these new ideas require a new campus master plan? List in chronological order all the steps that you will take in order to lead the community beyond this serious impasse.

Notes

1. Bryant and Sharer, *The CEO Test*, 11–35.
2. Dallavis, "Centralizing Data," 38–41.

The Strategic Plan as Institutional Road Map   47

3. For example, Wodon, "Heterogeneity in Parental Priorities," 178–205, and Wodon, "Catholic Higher Education Globally."

4. Avoid limiting the list of aspirant and peer schools to only other Catholic schools.

5. Mellul, *Post–COVID 19 World of Work and Study.* See also Douglas Belkin, "More Say Colleges Aren't Worth the Cost," *Wall Street Journal,* April 1–2, 2023.

6. Wodon, "Catholic Higher Education Globally," 8. See also Wodon, "Catholic Higher Education in the United States."

7. Grawe, *The Agile College,* 1. See also Grawe, *Demographics and the Demand*; and Fischer, "The Shrinking of Higher Ed."

8. See https://www.nces.ed.gov.

9. See also, Smith, "Data Dive," 47–49.

10. NCEA, *National Standards and Benchmarks,* 27–29.

11. Soghoian, *Mind the Gap!*

12. Rose and Large, *Higher Education Business Models,* 26.

13. Martin and James E. Samels & Associates, *Consolidating Colleges.*

14. LeBlanc and Clerkin, "A Disruptive Opportunity," 123–35.

15. Martin and James E. Samels & Associates, "Consolidation of American Higher Education," 3–13.

16. Hoyle, "If That Moment Arrives," 199–208.

17. While the origin of this quote is often debated, *Forbes* attributes the quote to Will Rogers. See www.forbes.com>quotes>thoughtsonthe businessoflife>willrogers.

18. Often a strategic plan will identify a goal to "conduct a campus master plan study" as part of its five-year institutional road map.

19. Flannery, *How to Market a University,* 1–18.

20. Bryant and Sharer, *The CEO Test,* 13–14.

21. If a school does not have the internal resources for such analysis, the tasks must be outsourced, as reliable data is an essential component of both strategic planning and overall responsible school management.

3

Fostering a Vibrant Community

Presidents set the tone for their communities when they consistently think in terms of "we" and unambiguously demonstrate the priority of fostering a safe, healthy school environment and an inclusive, versatile community.[1] High-impact leaders consistently highlight the accomplishments of community members, especially students, faculty, and staff; they understand that respect is not necessarily popularity; they are friendly without thinking of themselves as "friends" of employees or students.[2] This chapter explores the key characteristics of a vibrant academic community and offers specific steps that a president can take to promote such vitality, including efforts that foster student-centered facilities, promote academic excellence, recognize the invaluable role of dedicated faculty and staff, and encourage student leadership on local, regional, and global levels.

Characteristics of a Healthy School Culture

Multiple characteristics come to mind when describing a healthy school culture: a strong commitment to the mission and strategic goals; an environment of affirmation, mutual trust, civility in all discourse, honesty; and a firm belief in active intellectual inquiry. Within a healthy culture there is palpable happiness among the students and strong intellectual energy permeates the

Fostering a Vibrant Community 49

campus. In addition, vibrant communities foster a deep sense of accountability for everyone's responsibilities and engage in frequent communication. In such a climate, every member of the community feels respected and appreciated, with achievements recognized and celebrated.

Conversely, an unhealthy school environment can be genuinely toxic, exhibiting mistrust, disrespect, disloyalty, a lack of purpose or sense of gratitude, and a milieu of constant complaints and gossip. Such a climate is devoid of both happiness and energy. No educator wants to work in this kind of negative climate, as it directly impacts the quality of education and the morale of everyone in the community, including students, who are quick to perceive a hostile climate among teachers, staff, or administrators. Presidents who encounter this type of toxic environment must confront the situation immediately and do everything within their power—which is considerable—to reverse the tendency toward small-mindedness and negativity, neither of which has a place in an educational organization, classroom, or community that (by its very nature) is committed to open inquiry. Vibrant academic communities transcend narrow-minded pettiness in order to envision reality within broader, more robust contexts.

Fostering a Healthy School Community

While every Catholic school must determine for itself the ways in which its community will nurture a healthy climate and cultivate a vibrant culture, there are transcending qualities— practiced and promoted in Catholic schools throughout the world today—that characterize energetic academic environments.

What are these qualities, and how does an individual president foster a healthy school environment? While the following steps may seem obvious and simple to achieve, it is often possible to neglect some of them, given the fast pace of an academic year.

50   *Chapter 3*

Recognize the Importance of Ritual

A high-impact president appreciates the importance of rituals that gather members of the community in a meaningful way. These rituals can range from celebrating the Mass of the Holy Spirit to mark the beginning of the academic year, to the fitting elegance and solemnity of graduation ceremonies, or to smaller but equally meaningful rituals such as the school ring ceremony or events that recognize the efforts of student clubs or the success of athletic teams. However, even a simple practice such as starting the school day or classes with a brief prayer contributes to the powerful sense of "we."

Regardless of the scale, all ceremonies should be well-planned and executed with care. Sensitive leaders understand the quiet importance of these rituals and make every effort to provide these shared experiences frequently, as they strengthen and enhance the overall quality of community life.

Promote a Highly Collaborative Culture

A second way to generate a healthy school environment is to promote a highly consultative and collaborative climate (see chapters 1 and 2, on mission and strategic planning). The president should strive to achieve a broad level of community input in the varied organizational processes, including strategic planning, the formation of a campus master plan, preparations for accreditation visits, decisions related to the school's administrative/academic technologies, and the generation of new interdisciplinary programs on key areas such as wellness, diversity, equity, inclusion, and global leadership. While the president and the board of trustees must make the final decisions on the most serious matters, wide community input concerning major school issues is essential and invaluable.

This broad level of community consultation should include students, staff, faculty, trustees, parents, and alumni, with

Fostering a Vibrant Community 51

formats that can vary from formal survey instruments to town hall meetings to focus groups. The important point is that this collaborative model should be evident to the community at all times, with participation encouraged, acknowledged, and valued.

Create Attractive Environments

Assuming a highly safe environment, the Catholic school should also be a campus that is well-maintained, well-organized, bright, clean, and environmentally responsible—an atmosphere that both exudes student energy and creates a peaceful space for study and reflection. Such environments should characterize all classrooms but also the library/learning commons, student lounges, dining facilities, residence halls, and athletic facilities. Students should be able to immediately recognize that they are in a welcoming, special, and safe place.

During their tenures, savvy presidents will visit other schools, at least on a regional basis. These visits promote a collegial spirit, but more importantly they provide a window into how other campuses present themselves and function. A visiting leader can usually sense a welcoming space that offers gracious hospitality, versus one that is chaotic and disorganized—an impression usually evident at the very first point of interaction with the receptionist in the school's lobby or entrance to the administrative offices. Such visits often include a tour and help develop key insights concerning the school environment: Are student works of art and research efforts on display? Does the school offer comfortable spaces for student interactions and study groups? Is the environment bright and lively? Do the faculty and staff have adequate professional areas for collaboration? Do the dining facilities provide space for community interaction? Are the academic and administrative technologies state-of-the-art? These and many other signs provide a leader in education with ideas for improving her or his own school

52 Chapter 3

while indicating steps/decisions/choices to avoid. Site visits also demonstrate the importance of campus master planning and its emphasis on coordinated environments and well-maintained open spaces.

Recognize the Invaluable Role of Faculty and Staff

Frequent presidential recognition of the invaluable contributions of the faculty and the staff is exceptionally important, as these dedicated, highly reliable, hardworking, and trustworthy professionals deserve the school's deepest gratitude for their untiring efforts to help students. To demonstrate ongoing administrative support for their employees, high-impact presidents do not hesitate to pose to them some basic questions: How can I help you succeed? What resources do you need to fulfill your responsibilities? In addition to posing such open-ended questions to all employees (and responding as needed), successful presidents also demonstrate a commitment to providing frequent opportunities for the exercise of shared governance, as well as access to state-of-the-art technology, membership in professional learning communities and affinity groups, and opportunities to attend professional regional, national, and international conferences.[3] Successful presidents are especially attentive to the physical spaces offered to faculty and staff—including offices, lounges, and dining facilities. In addition, the academic year should include several structured social activities, such as a special luncheon to open the school year or an employee recognition dinner to celebrate anniversaries of service to the school.

Faculty and staff remain the "front line" of daily interaction with students, and a committed president has a serious responsibility to recognize and promote their indispensable role, especially because the leader has unique multiple opportunities to express this gratitude publicly, as when addressing the board

Fostering a Vibrant Community 53

of trustees, parents of students, alumni groups, or the wider community in which the school is situated. By consistently acknowledging the faculty and staff for their dedicated service to students, the president models a disposition of gratitude that ought to characterize the entire community.

Commit to Academic Excellence

Excellent academic quality is expected in a Catholic educational community, as it is an institution "distinguished by its free speech for the whole truth about nature, man, and God" and its belief "in the intrinsic value of knowledge and research."[4] In a focused manner, a high-impact president appreciates and celebrates the unique role of faculty, those women and men inspired by "academic ideals and by the principles of an authentically human life."[5] In the context of higher education, it should be abundantly clear to the faculty that the school's president understands and protects the "academic freedom of scholars in each discipline in accordance with its own principles and proper methods, and within the confines of the truth and the common good."[6]

The president should also understand that the quality of teaching is the most important factor impacting student persistence and success.[7] The successful president, therefore, expects that faculty practice a substantive, student-centered methodology in their classrooms and in all their interactions with students. This includes offering depth within the curriculum and strong interdisciplinary work that breaks down a "silo" approach to teaching and learning. In addition, academic excellence incorporates active, collaborative learning models; these may include inquiry-based learning, project-based learning, hybrid instructional modalities, small group instruction, and other methods that demonstrate an overall commitment to "best practice" teaching and ongoing assessment within a subject matter. While the specific teaching methodology remains the discretion of the individual faculty member, high-impact

54   *Chapter 3*

leaders make every effort to support all teaching approaches with the necessary resources.

Faculty typically need to help most students learn how to study, reflect, absorb, and understand academic material, as students come to realize that mastering academic subject matter is hard work and requires intellectual energy. Superficial thinking and the collapse of "truth" into the formulation of an opinion achieved without study, analysis, or reflection is a cultural temptation that students need to recognize and reject. By challenging students to excel and demonstrating confidence in their ability to do so, faculty set the academic bar high and signal their expectation of serious work. It is not unusual for students to express surprise at how much they can actually achieve when a teacher believes in their ability to accomplish greatness.

In addition to this quest for academic excellence, Catholic schools also are often highly creative in providing opportunities that knit an entire school or class into a single academic project. Often schools select a yearly school theme to provide a seamless, problem-solving learning opportunity for the entire student body. For example, all K-12 grade students can relate to the theme of "water" and may study this life-giving resource from the perspective of all disciplines, while a college or university may require first-year students to read a common text in order to explore its key themes during orientation sessions.

Today many schools—at all levels—are embracing school-wide curricular and cocurricular opportunities that explore social themes, such as engaged citizenship, the importance of civil discourse characterized by sincere dialogue and mutual respect, and the essential characteristics of a healthy democracy.[8] To address these pressing societal needs, Lincoln Snyder, president of NCEA, lists such topics among his "Four Calls to Action" by which Catholic K-12 schools can demonstrate genuine leadership in the wider society, as he notes the following:

> Our schools must lead in teaching and modeling discourse as foundational for civil society. We believe in the truth; we choose

our own curriculum; we believe in teaching logic, rhetoric and debate as the key to the pursuit of truth; we are not afraid to take countercultural positions; and we teach our students the same. Our commitment to these principles benefits society as a whole, especially at a time when so many institutions do not share that commitment.[9]

The Association of Governing Boards of Universities and Colleges (AGB) identified "civic education and democracy" as one of its top 2022–2023 strategic issues for academic leaders: "An institution of higher learning fails its students if it does not stir and prepare them to participate in civic life, to exercise their franchise, to form and express reasoned opinions, and to hear and consider the viewpoints of other people."[10] University demonstrations provoked by the recent Israel-Hamas war magnify this imperative that all academic institutions promote a civic engagement that presupposes informed participants and respectful discourse.[11]

Given the importance of using creative approaches to teaching, substantive course offerings, and time-sensitive themes, the high-impact president must also devote significant attention to key performance indicators concerning the school's academic quality and the students' overall ability to master critical competencies required for their next level of education, career, or role in society. These indicators include formal reports from accrediting bodies and external standardized tests administered by nationally recognized, discipline-based organizations.

Provide Substantive Cocurricular Offerings

To demonstrate the comprehensive scope of Catholic education, cocurricular activities indicate a student-centered approach that addresses the whole person. These activities include very intentional programs that promote multiple aspects of student wellness, including the physical, sexual, emotional, social, and intellectual aspects of the whole person; these can range from

56 *Chapter 3*

the basketball team to the chess club, to the photography club or pre-law mock trial team. The priority is to offer *substantive* activities that provide a wide range of options and experiences during which students develop interpersonal skills and move beyond their immediate circle of friends in order to mix with peers from throughout the school. Cocurricular activities also enable students to focus on issues about which they care deeply, such as protecting the environment, and to do so in a manner that addresses the multidimensional nature of the issue.

In faith-based Catholic schools, of course, the spiritual dimension is understood to be a critical part of this student experience, with intentional programs offered through campus ministry and other student life offices. (Chapter 1 on mission articulates some of these faith-based programs, such as liturgical celebrations, retreat opportunities, and service projects.)

Promote Student Leadership

A student-centered environment must include multiple leadership opportunities for students. In addition to student government positions, student leadership should be prominent in all cocurricular activities, including clubs, athletic teams, musical performances, art exhibits, and a host of other offerings. Adults who moderate student organizations, however, should not assume that every student knows what it means to be a leader. Efforts to provide in-depth leadership development opportunities on campus foster student empowerment, as do many professional organizations offering high-quality programs through regional and national conferences that give student leaders the opportunity to meet and work with a range of students from a wide geographical area who share similar interests and roles. Many religious orders or dioceses that sponsor schools also have strong networks that offer a range of student-focused experiences. In recent years many student leadership programs have emphasized the importance of creating inclusive, diverse

Fostering a Vibrant Community 57

communities by exploring religious, racial, cultural, political, and economic differences, to cite just a few areas—all within the context of the core Catholic principle of valuing the innate human dignity of every person.

Encourage/Assess Student Participation

As educators know, continual student participation in the richness of school life is essential. In addition to active class attendance, cocurricular activities serve as a key performance indicator of student engagement. When attentive faculty, staff, and administrators identify those students who fail to attend or participate in their selected curricular and cocurricular activities, the school's professional counselors should follow up and address these isolation issues as soon as possible, since these behaviors are often symptomatic of other serious underlying problems and often become worse if neglected. In recent years these counseling opportunities and wellness programs have grown in importance, as some children and young adults may struggle with questions concerning sexuality or directly experience cyberbullying, violence in the home, eating disorders, discrimination, cutting, consumption of alcohol and drugs, rape, depression, or thoughts of suicide.

As the AGB notes in its *Top Strategic Issues for Boards 2022–2023,* "Students' mental, physical, social, and emotional needs are greater than ever before. Compounding the issue is that some students—especially those at most risk of failure—may have suffered significant learning loss during the pandemic. Colleges need to bring those students up to speed rapidly and be ready to respond if they show any signs of emotional distress."[12] By bringing together counselors, health care professionals, campus ministry, student life administrators, and other resources, Catholic schools emphasize that they are "safe harbors" and places of understanding, support, healing, hope, and belonging for all students.[13]

58   *Chapter 3*

Broaden Student Horizons

A key part of engagement introduces students to the "city as classroom" concept, which utilizes all the cultural resources within the school's specific region, including art museums, musical concerts, and film institutes. In addition, the immediate geographical area affords sites for meaningful supervised service and internship experiences.

Students should also be encouraged to see themselves as global citizens with the "world as a classroom."[14] Carefully vetted and well-planned opportunities for international academic exchanges and service experiences promote joint learning opportunities that foster intercultural understanding and provide students with life-changing opportunities. At the college and university levels, there are multiple research areas and service opportunities within a cross-cultural international context that genuinely enhance the common good. These include strengthening nutritional options and promoting clean drinking water. Alumni often mention these experiences when reflecting on pivotal moments in their educational experiences; they are grateful that their alma mater understood the importance of offering global perspectives and cross-cultural immersion opportunities in a highly complex, often fragmented world.

Prioritize Interaction with Students

Successful presidents understand that their leadership position— filled with committee meetings, alumni engagements, board of trustees consultations, and the countless other responsibilities— often remove them from frequent and direct student contact, and they therefore prioritize interactions with students by carefully structuring opportunities to meet them. While informal encounters with students may occur on a daily basis in a school corridor or at athletic events and other venues, a more formal approach that carefully schedules and promotes president-student conversations allows leaders to hear from the students directly. These events might include breakfasts or lunches, town hall meetings, and focus groups. What are students thinking about current events? What are their concerns? How can the school improve in order to enhance their experience?

Administrators learn a great deal from this unfiltered student exchange that encourages students to speak openly and honestly. A word of caution, however: too often administrators are tempted to dominate these meetings, using the opportunity to promote the school's successes or future plans. Sensitive leaders understand the importance of carefully listening to students, as these meetings are unique opportunities for the students to voice their ideas and concerns directly to the school's president. Student topics may range from transportation issues to resident hall resources, to curricular offerings, to the cafeteria menu; while not all issues presented by students may have an easy solution, some topics can be immediately addressed, signaling that the school's leader genuinely listens and takes students seriously. These presidential initiatives signal a clear message: students are heard; their experiences are respected; their voices count; their ideas are always welcome.

Foster Safe Environments for Students

A school president assumes a serious moral and legal obligation to provide a safe environment for all students entrusted to their care. All K-12 students deserve a safe educational environment and community in which they feel protected. It is important to note that the school president is responsible for implementing all federal and state laws and regulations regarding the obligations of K-12 educators to protect minors, including each state's specific instructions on mandated reporting and the professional training and certification that is required (see chapter 4 regarding risk assessment and crisis management).

Likewise, college and university students must have confidence that all sections of their campus are safe, including residence halls and parking lots, regardless of the time of day or

60   *Chapter 3*

night. While most colleges and universities have a dedicated campus safety or police department, as well as a health / counseling / wellness center, all teachers and staff who work in higher education must remain attentive to suspected abuse. Students with multiple bruises, frequent absences, a tendency to isolate, and other signs of distress may indicate that a student is in serious physical or psychological trouble and should be immediately reported by the faculty or staff member to the appropriate college/university official. The school, as a safe harbor, also protects those students who may feel marginalized, including students of color or LGBTQ+ students. By virtue of their mission, Catholic schools are faith-based communities in which all students are respected and treated humanely, with their human dignity acknowledged and their essential human goodness as God's children cherished. High-impact leaders work tirelessly to promote these values that pertain to every member of the community by upholding a zero-tolerance policy concerning hateful and discriminating words and actions.

Likewise, many students today describe a certain loneliness, alienation, and general lack of meaning and loss of purpose in their lives—an ironic situation, given that there are more ways to communicate today than ever before in human history. Despite the quantity of social media platforms that provide unabated waves of information and opportunities for interaction, certain students experience detachment, loneliness, isolation, or pain. To address this troubling reality, many schools dedicate significant time and effort to teaching proper social media etiquette, including the malicious nature of cyberbullying. Such sessions, often provided by a school's wellness or counseling center, should be readily available for all students, with special attention to those who struggle.

All students will remember at least some parts of their highly formative school years. Indelible impressions are made, whether students participate in student government, rank academically high, immerse themselves in international cross-cultural experiences, or participate in theater or sports. Did they have a positive experience? Were they respected and treated with kindness? Were the teachers and staff available when they needed help? Did they experience high-quality teaching and meaningful classes? Did they experience abundant leadership opportunities and a wide range of cocurricular activities? Did the learning experience extend beyond the traditional classroom? Did they find learning challenging and engaging? Were they well-prepared for the next stage of their life?

Promote Parent Engagement: K-12 Students

As the primary educators of their children, most parents of K-12 students want to be highly involved in their children's educational experience, especially since the COVID-19 pandemic.[15] Every president must balance parental interest with parental overreach. An effective way to achieve this balance is to have a close working relationship with the leaders of the parents' association, especially its executive committee. These professional opportunities provide the conduit for a steady exchange of information with the school's leader and usually include regularly scheduled "parental feedback" sessions on a wide range of issues that parents deem to be priorities.

In addition, small group meetings with parents are highly effective, and sessions can be organized by class or activity (for example, performing arts, athletics, student government). These opportunities provide focused feedback to presidents. Whether held on campus or hosted by parents in their homes, such gatherings also provide leaders the opportunity to disseminate information designed to meet the specific interests of each group. Is construction of a new track field in the campus master plan? What performing arts programs are planned for the future? Are there specific international service trips that will be undertaken in the next academic semester?

An additional means for president-parent interaction is a "state of the school" address, which creates a unique opportunity to disseminate timely information deemed to be highly

62   *Chapter 3*

important. It is also the moment to express a message of hope for the school's future and one's ability to lead the school into that future. When concluding this address, the president should open the session to questions from the audience, as this demonstrates the ability to exhibit presidential confidence and extensive knowledge concerning the school. School leaders should not be surprised with questions, which can range from projected tuition increases to parking congestion to a lack of certain class offerings.

The key to all these different formats is making oneself available. Parents appreciate presidents who are communicating with them regularly and who are attentive to their concerns. Parents also appreciate presidents who address pressing issues quickly and without fanfare, and who provide regular updates on the solutions to longer-term problems. Parents of children in K-12 Catholic schools have many educational choices, and many make significant sacrifices to send their children to faith-based academic communities. Keeping parents respectfully engaged strengthens the school community and constitutes another key dimension to realizing a vibrant educational environment.

Promote Parent Engagement: College and University Students

While college and university administrators do not experience intense parental involvement by undergraduates' parents, there are important opportunities for a high level of presidential visibility in order to connect directly with parents, especially as first-year and transfer students join the school community. Orientation days often include the opening of residence halls as well as various celebrations, including the liturgy. Homecoming and various athletic and cultural events throughout the academic year may attract attendance by parents, as does the annual family weekend, often held in the fall. All these opportunities provide presidents with important moments to promote the Catholic mission of the college or university and its

Fostering a Vibrant Community 63

commitment to a faith-based environment that upholds values such as honesty, courage, generosity, kindness, and respect, a message that parents often find reassuring. In addition, a president's emphasis on student safety, the quality of the faculty, the range of academic programs, and the importance of community ensures parents that their daughter or son has found a safe second home.

Develop Strong Senior Leadership Teams

To foster a vibrant, healthy community, presidents have a special obligation to identify and develop leadership within and throughout the school. This is especially true of the senior leadership team (at times called a cabinet, core team, or similar title), members of the community who directly report to the school's leader on a daily basis and who also function as key administrators in a school emergency. They are leaders in their own right who should be respected and valued.

High-impact presidents set the bar high and expect exceptional performance from their senior leadership teams. These women and men should be "subject matter" experts in their areas of responsibility and display both the expertise and the experience needed to lead their respective faculty and staff in fulfilling the school's mission and strategic plan. However, presidents also know the value of frequent expressions of gratitude to all members of this senior team, for these administrators work hard and contribute long hours on any given day. The annual "senior leadership team retreat" off campus or a special cabinet luncheon are examples of simple presidential actions that express appreciation for dedicated service.

Presidents expect their immediate leadership team to be loyal, to understand the concept of working as a team, and to respect confidentiality at all times. While there should be adequate time for debate and disagreement within the team, such disputes should be restricted to cabinet meetings that are regularly scheduled, well-organized meetings chaired by the president. During

64   *Chapter 3*

such meetings, serious confidential discussions should explore various perspectives on a particular issue, with the assumption that everyone arrives at the meeting fully prepared to address specific agenda topics. In these types of environments, team members must listen carefully to one another (without distractions) and pertinent information should neither be withheld nor deliberately blurred in order to "protect" the president. During these sessions, presidents too must actively listen, since they are seeking advice from their senior team and should reflect a genuine openness to different perspectives.[16] They can also never assume that "no news is good news." Successful leaders do not like surprises, whether the news is good or bad. For this reason, presidents need unfiltered information, for only when they are fully informed can situations be promptly and properly addressed. In the most serious cases, the president may need to take the issue directly to the board of trustees.

Debate, disagreement, and discussion, however, end at the door. In the wider school community, senior leaders need to project a unified voice and support all executive decisions and their implementation. There can be no betrayal of confidentiality or disclosure of the details of the meetings or various positions held by certain team members. Such a breach of trust is a failure in loyalty and the concept of teamwork, and the president must address any such breach immediately in order to protect the integrity of the process, the overall functioning of the senior leadership team, and the well-being of the entire school.[17]

High-impact leaders know the value of subsidiarity and delegation. They respect the knowledge of their team members and do not attempt to micromanage these individuals. Micromanaging should not be necessary and is never desirable, as routine presidential intervention undermines the credibility of the senior leadership team, absorbs a disproportionate amount of time and energy, and distracts everyone from their unique responsibilities. Frequent occasions of micromanagement also demoralize senior leaders, especially if this type of overinvolvement is viewed as unnecessary or intrusive.

Successful leaders inspire, energize, and empower senior team members to achieve personal and professional success by providing clear expectations and honest, ongoing performance discussions that evaluate accomplishments and explore new ideas. These review sessions also offer presidents the opportunity to affirm a job well done or address problems of concern. The overall goal is always professional growth—a growth that includes expertise, experience, accountability, teamwork, and mutual respect. Moreover, senior administrators hold a serious level of responsibility in the school; they should be compensated appropriately and provided with frequent professional development opportunities financed by the school.

Presidents often reflect on their senior leadership teams with a great sense of pride and deep gratitude for their collaborative spirit, their service to the school community, and their indispensable insights and expertise. A certain bond of mutual respect exists, especially since the cabinet team spends a great deal of time together, with members coming to know one another well. For this reason, mentorship of senior leaders is always a profound privilege for any president, who understands and appreciates the immeasurable impact of careful succession planning in order to prepare the next generation of presidential leadership.

Hire for Mission

A healthy school community presupposes a deeply committed faculty, staff, administrators, and strong leadership team, which underscores the importance of the hiring process. The significance of hiring for mission cannot be overstated, as those employed by the school have a significant impact on the community's ability to fulfill its educational commitments in the context of faith.[18] Many teachers and staff remain at one school for the entirety of their career, thereby influencing generations of students and making an indelible mark on the school's history. They are a living testimony to the vibrant and enduring

66   *Chapter 3*

nature of the Catholic mission. Whether the school uses national or regional search firms or oversees the process internally, a president must recognize the importance of this opportunity and dedicate the appropriate time and resources to this hiring process. Catholic schools are highly competitive when it comes to hiring qualified teachers and staff, and it is incumbent on a president to advocate before the board for the most competitive salaries possible, with appropriate salary increases projected every year. Hiring employees who will contribute to the mission and who also demonstrate appropriate professional qualifications is one of the most important presidential responsibilities, given that this decision may impact multiple classes of students for many years.

In addition to assessing "mission fit" as a criterion for hiring, senior administrators must also determine the actual need for a new position or a replacement hire when a division head or dean brings such a request forward. Academic institutions can easily overstaff, becoming bloated and inefficient. On the other hand, a school cannot function properly if it is understaffed and unable to meet its operating requirements. A lean, uncomplicated, but high-quality academic community is ideal, as it reflects both effectiveness and efficiency.

Other questions regarding the initial position request are also central: How does this position link to the school's strategic plan? What are the appropriate, competencies required for this position? Who should comprise a representative search committee? How will the initial interview process be conducted—virtually or in person? How will the school ensure fairness and integrity throughout the search?

While the school community deserves transparency concerning the hiring process of the search, a president retains responsibility for all confidential matters related to offering an appropriate and competitive salary, given the specific candidate's credentials and employment history as well as other personal matters that may surface during the interview process. The president must also secure a fully executed contract in a

Fostering a Vibrant Community 67

timely fashion, often with the advice of legal counsel, although at many colleges and universities this responsibility can be delegated to a vice president or dean. The president's signature, however, usually appears on the letter of employment, as he or she bears ultimate responsibility for the quality of the school's employees.

Prioritize Employee Professional Development and Retention

Once a new person is hired, the president assumes a professional relationship with the employee that obliges both employer and employee to a high level of accountability and mutual respect, and a high-impact president is vigilant in promoting employee success and job satisfaction. For instance, is the teaching or office environment safe and conducive to productive professional work? Does the employee have access to appropriate, well-maintained technology? Are adequate professional development opportunities provided for all faculty and staff, especially on mission-related topics such as the Catholic intellectual tradition or the specific history of the school in which the employee serves?[19] Do these enrichment opportunities include campus-based programs as well as external regional, national, and international opportunities? Is there a process by which the employee (in coordination with the supervisor) establishes yearly goals that include a focus on mission and strategic planning priorities as well as on discipline-specific responsibilities? Are assessment tools in place to evaluate an employee's goal realization and effectiveness? Does the administration provide the employee with ongoing evaluations and honest feedback versus the "annual spring review"?

Regardless of the size of the institution, it is essential to have a strong human resources office (often situated in the finance office) to oversee employee onboarding, address certain employee issues, and provide a user-friendly means for employees to engage with the institution (e.g., being able to review their

68   *Chapter 3*

benefits using a secure tracking software that provides clear snapshots of available vacation days, sick days, and other benefits). Equally essential is a comprehensive employee handbook that documents all school policies and procedures and is updated each year with the advice of legal counsel. Principles that are mandated should be clearly distinguished from those that are recommendations only, and the handbook should include a code of ethics that unambiguously states regulations concerning employee behavior, especially when interacting with students. No matter how collegial the Catholic academic community may be (often describing itself as a "family"—a title that can blur reality), faculty and staff are involved in a contractual business relationship that must be understood, respected, and fulfilled, with mutual accountability upheld.

While most employees execute their responsibilities faithfully, difficult personnel decisions, however, do arise and one of the most challenging presidential responsibilities centers on addressing these situations, as when an employee fails to honor expected professional obligations in some manner. In every case, due process and fairness must be the norm, with performance failures addressed forthrightly and justly. Failure on the part of the employee to fulfill a contract cannot be ignored, as problems tend to fester, sometimes worsen, and negatively impact the wider school environment. How serious is the matter? Is this a first-time occasion or indicative of a pattern of irresponsibility? Is a verbal or written warning an appropriate response, or is the matter so serious that the behavior warrants termination after careful exercise of due process has exhausted all other forms of discipline? Presidents agonize over these questions and never make disciplinary decisions lightly. Choosing to place an employee on a professional plan for improvement or suspending or terminating an employee are some of the most difficult decisions for all presidents, who often agonize over decisions that affect an employee's reputation and career. Is there a justified and well-documented case for taking action? Has the employee been fairly treated? Is the penalty commensurate with the contractual failure? Has confidentiality been upheld? These questions and many more reflect the thinking of a leader who assumes this responsibility with careful thought, due diligence, honesty, and fairness.

Conclusion

There are numerous ways by which a high-impact leader can foster a vibrant, healthy school community and create a quality of life that should be evident in the school's mission, reflected in the school's strategic plan, and experienced daily on the campus. While the president delegates the actual planning and implementation of all community-based experiences, it is important that the president ensures that every experience is offered in a thoughtful, well-designed manner. All members of the community, as well as external agencies such as accrediting bodies, expect to see a style of leadership that is consistently dedicated to strengthening the community and enhancing the educational experience and overall quality of life on campus.

A flourishing teaching and learning environment protects student safety and promotes academic excellence. It recognizes the accomplishments of the faculty and staff, appreciates parental input, and respects the significant investment parents have made in the school to which they have entrusted their daughters and sons. With all these constituencies, a president holds a unique and highly visible responsibility to promote the success of every community member, and when exercised well, this model of leadership leaves a lasting and immeasurable mark on the community's overall well-being and daily experience.

How to Foster a Vibrant Academic Community

- Use every gathering, large or small, as an opportunity to express the school's commitment to creating a safe, vibrant, and inclusive community.
- Demonstrate an unwavering commitment to a collaborative

70   *Chapter 3*

model of leadership by offering frequent and well-planned opportunities for all school constituencies.

- Commit to maintaining a lively, well-organized school environment that promotes and celebrates student and faculty achievements.
- Expect academic excellence across all disciplines and offer substantive, well-planned cocurricular programs that offer a wide range of opportunities for students; continually assess these programs' effectiveness, especially in the area of student engagement.
- Offer formal programs that promote the development of student leadership skills and provide multiple opportunities for students to exercise that leadership.
- Prioritize frequent interactions with students in all activities (athletic events, art exhibits, club presentations, and academic award ceremonies, to cite a few).
- Hire for mission and treat all employees with dignity and fairness; recognize and promote the invaluable role of the faculty and the staff.
- Foster a safe environment through rigorous compliance with all federal and state laws regarding the protection of minors. Ensure that all students in the school community feel safe and supported.
- Express gratitude to parents for their trust and investment.
- Build strong leadership teams, especially by providing multiple professional development opportunities.

Key Questions

1. This chapter explores important aspects of a vibrant school culture/community. What other aspects would you add? Think about your present Catholic school culture: How would you describe this culture?

2. Is your school culture healthy? If yes, in what ways is this so?

3. Is your school culture unhealthy? If yes, in what ways is this so?

Fostering a Vibrant Community 71

4. At your present school what curricular or cocurricular programs for students are especially successful? Why are these programs so successful?

5. Does your school offer courses and seminars on civil discourse and the role of citizenship in a democracy? Does your school address the issue of cyberbullying?

6. In what ways can your school be improved to ensure more faculty and staff engagement and overall professional fulfillment?

7. How active are parent groups within your school? Do you participate in any school-wide social events sponsored by the parents?

8. If a new president, what steps would you take to introduce yourself to your new academic community?

9. If a new president, what steps would you take to introduce yourself to the wider, more public community in which the school is situated (township, city, county, business group, academic association, or other entity)?

10. How can trustees assist a new president's integration into the school and wider community?

Case Study: Fostering a Vibrant Community

You learn in late November that your chief academic officer (provost, principal) is leaving the school at the end of the current academic year in order to assume a presidency in another state. This move immediately opens a key administrative position that needs to be filled by mid-August at the very latest.

At your request, the board of trustees approves the use of a national firm to conduct the search process. While the school's bylaws do not require the chief academic officer to be a practicing Catholic, initial conversations with the entire school community make clear that a commitment to Catholic mission and identity, as well as a strong strategic vision and extensive administrative experience, are expected in this role. Appropriate academic credentials and a stellar academic record are also

72   *Chapter 3*

prerequisites. These expectations match your own concerning this role.

The consultant who will oversee the process visits campus to conduct focus groups with all community members who have registered for these opinion-gathering sessions. The consultant holds separate meetings with you, as well as with members of your senior leadership team (excluding the current provost or principal), with deans and program directors, with officers from the faculty senate, and with student government leaders. A representative search committee appointed by you also meets with the consultant for an extended period of time. This first phase of consultation produces a robust position description that you ultimately approve. In turn, these search-related documents are posted on the school's website and on the search firm's "open positions" listing.

By now spring break is fast approaching, so the search is "fast-tracked" in order to invite three finalists to campus who have been culled from a larger pool that has already been interviewed by the search committee via video conference. Once the search firm completes reference checks, campus visits are planned to meet the three candidates in multiple settings over a two-day period; campus visits include a private meeting with you and a separate meeting with the academic leadership. An e-survey feedback form is posted on your school's website for anyone who wants to provide responses after attending any of several presentation sessions open to students, faculty, and staff (meetings that are also simultaneously broadcast via your school's secure network).

After community feedback is conscientiously tallied, one finalist emerges as the consensus candidate by the majority of the school community. After the search firm conducts additional background checks on the candidate, this individual is invited to an off-campus interview with you, the board chair, and other members of the board's executive committee. This is the final step in the interview process before a formal employment offer is made and includes the opportunity for the candidate to ask her or his own questions.

Fostering a Vibrant Community 73

While it is evident in the meeting that board members are exceptionally pleased with this finalist, you have started to have doubts about the "fit" of the candidate. Several questions persist in your mind and have disturbed you since your earlier private meeting with the candidate; they have also surfaced again during this interview session with the trustees. These issues center around Catholic identity. It appears to you that certain terms used by the candidate reflect a lack of understanding of the actual meanings of those terms. You begin to suspect that the finalist may have carefully rehearsed these responses. When pressed with your follow-up questions concerning Catholic education and how a leader protects and promotes academic freedom within a Catholic context, the candidate seems flustered. The meeting adjourns and the finalist is taken to the nearby hotel where the school hosts its guests.

The following morning you meet with the board chair and all trustees who have interviewed the candidate at a session that everyone presumes will be the final step in the search process. Given the survey feedback, reference checks, and other elements of the process, the entire community seems to support this candidate. The trustees are especially pleased, given the individual's academic credentials and experience.

What do you do? Do you take a firm position against this finalist? Do you defer and trust the opinions of the trustees and the broader community? How do you specifically address your misgivings with the board chair? What other steps might be an appropriate course of action, given the rapidly approaching new academic year? Furthermore, upon reflection, was the search conducted carefully? Could the process have been improved? If so, how?

Notes

1. Drucker, "What Makes an Effective Executive," 62.
2. Dierickx, "Boundaries," in *High-Stakes Leadership*, 72–75.
3. Bahls, *Shared Governance*; Spillane, *Distributed Leadership*; DeFlaminis, Abdul-Jabbar, and Yoak, *Distributed Leadership in Schools*.
4. Pope John Paul II, *Apostolic Constitution*, 4, 15.

74 *Chapter 3*

5. Pope John Paul II, 22.
6. Pope John Paul II, 29; see also 12.
7. See, for instance, Gyurko et al., *Why Colleges*; Brown and Kurzweil, *Instructional Quality*; NCEA, *National Standards*.
8. Pope John Paul II, *Apostolic Constitution*, 21.
9. Snyder, "The Journey Ahead," 24.
10. AGB, *Top Strategic Issues*, 26.
11. See Joseph Ax and Gabriella Borter, "US Colleges Become Flashpoints for Protests over Israel-Hamas War," *Reuters*, October 14, 2023; Jack Stripling and Laura Meckler, "At Colleges, Violence in Israel and Gaza Ignites a War of Words," *Washington Post,* October 11, 2023; Michael R. Bloomberg, "Hamas's Barbarity Heightens the Crisis in Higher Education," *Wall Street Journal,* November 18, 2023, A13.
12. AGB, *Top Strategic Issues*, 20.
13. See Galvan, "NCEA Rise," 14–16.
14. This "world as classroom" approach is shaped by the relational model, not the typical business model that uses financial incentives to recruit and enroll students at American schools. The relational model identifies academic and cultural exchange sites on the basis of mission fit, location, safety, academic quality, and other significant criteria.
15. NCEA, *National Standards*, 9–10; Dallavis, "Fostering Parent Involvement."
16. Wawzenek, "Hear Me Out," 17–21.
17. See Bryant and Sharer, *The CEO Test*, 63–89.
18. NCEA, *National Standards*, 11–15; Earl, "Building Catholic Identity."
19. Holtschneider, "Treasure in Earthen Vessel," 20–34.

4

Risk Assessment and Crisis Management

LEADERS DO NOT GET TO CHOOSE THEIR CRISES. Moments that threaten school safety or signal danger to the community often come in unexpected ways and from unanticipated sources. Terrence MacTaggart's *Crisis Leadership for Boards and Presidents: Anticipating, Managing, and Leading Beyond Pandemics, Disruptions, and Ethical Failures* defines the situation as follows: "A crisis is a disruption to the stature, reputation, operations, and competitive position of a college, university, or system. Crises often ignite public scorn and call into question leaders' competence and integrity due to failures to anticipate, address, and lead through the crisis to a more positive outcome."[1] How do high-impact leaders prepare for crises within their schools? How do they navigate a wider community crisis that impacts school safety? What leadership qualities are required when a crisis occurs, especially as presidents bear ultimate responsibility for the safety of their school?

Covid-19 Pandemic: Lessons Learned

At this writing the United States continues to experience COVID-related hospitalizations and deaths, although numbers have significantly decreased from those experienced in 2020

76 *Chapter 4*

and 2021.[2] After several years of the pandemic, vaccines are now widely available, as are booster shots, oral antiviral medications, and home testing kits that ascertain the presence of COVID. Accelerated epidemiological research and vaccine development continues.[3]

However, it is a well-known fact that the pandemic negatively impacted education dramatically, and heated debate continues among parents' groups, associations of teachers, the media, and a wide range of politicians concerning the effects of the pandemic and the educational changes needed in its wake. Some groups point to early studies on the psychological, emotional, and intellectual effects of the pandemic.[4] Others debate the proper role of federal and state government in light of this experience.[5] This chapter highlights several lessons learned (from a presidential perspective) that draw from the two clear phases that schools experienced: (a) The closing of schools mandated by the governors of all fifty states at some point during the pandemic, a directive that immediately challenged leaders to manage the transition to virtual instruction, often with only a few days' notice;[6] and (b) the transition back to in-person education once it was deemed safe to do so by public health and state officials. From both phases of the pandemic, high-impact presidents can glean several specific lessons that reveal new dimensions of leadership and prompt fresh ways to provide high-quality education.

Adopt a Pastoral Role

The unparalleled emergency of the pandemic demonstrated the unique pastoral role that a president assumes in the face of such serious uncertainty, fear, and grief. During those intense pandemic years, effective presidents immediately put aside their own anxieties to bring a healing presence to an entire community. Faculty, staff, and students lost family members, friends, or neighbors during COVID-19, while some were hospitalized themselves. Many students experienced total isolation from their grandparents, encountering this type of separation for the first time in their lives. Adult emotions ranged from frustration to anger. School presidents who provided a steady, empathetic presence and message throughout this time reflected the type of compassion called for during such an extraordinary moment. They did not hesitate to ask the wider school community: What does our Catholic faith and mission bring to this situation? How can the community come together in prayer for the dying and all who are ill? How do students reach out to others with encouraging words during a quarantine period or when socially distancing in the school corridors?

Concentrate on Student Wholeness

The comprehensive well-being of students at every level—spiritual, intellectual, social, physical, and emotional—became a clear priority during the pandemic, and this integrated view remains of paramount importance in Catholic schools today. High-impact presidents took the lead in this area, ensuring the availability of centers of wellness that provide quiet meditation, mindfulness moments, nutritional education, and many other opportunities to help students address their feelings of isolation and the overall stresses of life that were magnified during the early pandemic years. These centers often bring together professional teams from counseling, health, physical education, and campus ministry departments in order to offer a comprehensive approach to community health.

Question a "Normal" Academic Experience

The pandemic prompted all presidents and educators to reconsider what constitutes a "normal" academic experience. Throughout the pandemic, K-12 faculty and staff adhered as closely as possible to the academic schedule, offered modified cocurricular activities, and scheduled parent/teacher sessions, while college professors kept the flow of the semester with

78   Chapter 4

integrated lectures, class discussions, student research papers, and presentations. All presidents and educators kept a keen eye on students scheduled to graduate, especially in 2020. Yet a question persisted throughout this intense experience: Is this the best way to offer a high-quality academic experience? This fundamental question includes topics that range from grading, assessment measures, attendance policies, the overall academic schedule, and employee responsibilities and workflow.

For example, in their essay, "The Post-Covid-19 Era: What Future and New Presidents Might Consider," James Soto Antony, Ana Mari Cauce, Lynn M. Gangone, and Tara P. Nicola note the following:

> Amid all the pain and very real devastation, there have been silver linings and lessons learned that will make for a stronger future. Unprecedented levels of creativity have been unleashed, and new ways of working and learning have emerged. And though while we write this, the pandemic is not yet over, higher education leaders are already asking themselves which practices, enacted under the most difficult circumstances imaginable, will they keep, at least in some form. Many are considering allowing some staff members to work remotely for a day or two or in some areas indefinitely. . . . We are asking ourselves whether we should be incorporating more remote learning not as a necessity but as another way of enhancing learning and flexibility for some students—whether in a 'flipped classroom' or hybrid format, such as having both remote and in-person study sections. It is not unreasonable to assume that in the future, all instructors will be expected to incorporate technology into their pedagogy and be able to adeptly move to class online during emergencies, making 'snow days' a thing of the past. We are questioning whether we need to travel as often for business and professional meetings.[7]

As a result of the COVID-19 experience, many Catholic K-12 schools are now implementing substantive changes in their educational approach. These include scheduling adjustments that reduce the number of classes each day while also extending class periods and the development of new models of parental engagement in the student learning experience, to cite two examples of a deliberate shift from pre-pandemic operational models.[8] One can only surmise that the immediate years ahead will witness many more innovative developments accelerated by the unprecedented pandemic disruption.

Focus on Technological Readiness and "Best Practice" in Pedagogy

Be prepared. Too many schools were unprepared for the arrival of COVID-19. When suddenly ordered to close (in spring 2020), too few schools demonstrated the nimbleness to handle the abrupt change. Did the school have the correct technological resources in place to make this rapid adjustment in a seamless way? Had pedagogy kept abreast of more flexible models? It was clear rather quickly that Catholic schools already possessing a high level of technological sophistication and experience fared far better in the initial months of the pandemic than those caught lacking this readiness. Schools that had existing 1:1 laptop programs and corresponding teacher readiness were already comfortable in the digital world and able to manage the crisis somewhat seamlessly in terms of necessary tools and methodology. By offering steady class schedules and access to digital library resources, as well as hosting study groups, providing cocurricular activities, and being available for individual student appointments, these schools realized successful outcomes, all accomplished remotely but effectively. Students and teachers were confident in this virtual world, although perhaps not on such a regular basis—all-day, every day instruction—and these schools achieved a level of teaching and learning effectiveness that exceeded other schools that were unprepared for a rapid digital transition.

Schools caught without the technological and pedagogical resources already functioning scrambled to secure laptops

80   Chapter 4

and teacher professional development opportunities in order to pivot quickly into this different online education delivery model. Precious class time and instruction were lost. A sense of insecurity in this unfamiliar virtual area dominated. Schools risked rising levels of student apathy and lowering numbers in classroom attendance. Although it is difficult to imagine any Catholic school president who did not pivot and change course as readily as possible and to the best of the school's ability, the seriousness of the situation clearly demonstrated that certain schools were unprepared for emergencies of this nature.

Embrace a Steep Learning Curve

In addition to concern about the reliability of the technology and faculty readiness, presidents and other senior administrators needed to immerse themselves immediately in the field of public health. School leaders found themselves on video conferences or webinar sessions with physicians and other healthcare experts, especially those who specialized in public health issues. Consultation with legal experts also increased dramatically throughout the pandemic as presidents dealt with the quickly unfolding pronouncements by the federal Centers for Disease Control and Prevention (CDC), as well as declarations by local officials, including their governor's offices and directors of public health within the specific state and county in which the school was located.

These regular medical and legal consultations were critical, in that parents and students frequently asked a range of questions concerning return to in-person instruction on campus, plans for graduation, and other end-of-academic year festivities. Schools were frequently compared: "School X is doing this; why can't our school do that too?" Intense pressure to change course often occurred, taxing the resolve of the most experienced president. In these cases, having real-time data and other empirical tools fortified any decisions, even as emotions ran high.

The enduring lesson is that these wider networks are an

Risk Assessment and Crisis Management 81

invaluable element of any successful school system, and effective leaders maintain ongoing contact with these professional groups, either through the president's office or delegated to an appropriate administrator. Hosting sessions that periodically gather this network on campus or via teleconference also strengthens the relationship and ensures that the educational voice is part of any public health planning in anticipation of the next major crisis that may confront the regional, national, or global communities.

Prioritize Communication

When professional organizations such as the National Academies of Sciences, Engineering, and Medicine and the American Academy of Pediatrics weighed health risks against the long-term academic, social, and psychological consequences of students continuing to miss in-person instruction, they concluded that schools should prioritize reopening as soon as possible, especially the early grades.[9] Many governors agreed, and they declared that public school districts, as well as private and parochial schools and all colleges and universities within their states, could determine their readiness to reopen, provided that appropriate safety protocols were followed. As a result, many Catholic K-12 schools elected to reopen for in-person instruction in the fall of 2020 after a summer of intense preparation.[10]

This decision prompted many presidents to take a fresh approach to communication— its delivery modes, the content, and the formats used—which they now use on a regular basis. During the most unstable pandemic period, especially when vaccines were not available to the public yet many K-12 Catholic schools were open, some presidents employed websites, videos, email and text blasts, church bulletins, podcasts, and other methods of delivery to communicate their pandemic policies, protocols that would be followed for contact tracing, and evolving safety plans. The emphasis was on timing and accuracy, given the evolving nature of the pandemic. It was equally

82   *Chapter 4*

important to regularly assess the effectiveness of all presidential communications, as the pace was often rapid and school policies and protocols were continually updated as needed.

Reexamine Physical Space

Effective presidents look at space differently, given the knowledge gained during the pandemic. The importance of careful campus master planning cannot be overstated, but the pandemic yielded a new appreciation of ample building ventilation, availability of hand sanitizer, fully equipped and staffed health centers, and cleaning procedures using appropriate disinfectant products. Physical adjustments allowing more space for students, especially in residence halls, have also become the norm.

Value the Role of the Board of Trustees

Presidents and trustees interacted far more frequently than usual in the early years of the pandemic. Effective presidents regularly sought the advice and authorization of the board prior to announcing any school policy related to COVID-19, as the safety risks were high and the consequences of decisions extraordinarily serious. Lives were at stake, and presidents and trustees alike felt that weight for many months. They realized that responsibility for providing a safe school environment ultimately fell to them, even as they sought regular advice from legal counsel, medical and public health professionals, and county, state, and federal officials. Trustee counsel and support throughout this intense period directly influenced the quality of a school's response to the pandemic and forged strong president-board relationships that will be felt years beyond the pandemic crisis.

COVID-19: Concluding Thoughts

Most educators agree that the pandemic left an indelible mark on education. Positive developments did occur, even when uncertainty gripped the national and international community, especially throughout the 2019–2020 and 2020–2021 academic years.[11] The vast majority of Catholic communities rose to the occasion and provided excellent online or in-person educational experiences to students, even within the mandated context of mask-wearing and social distancing. It is widely recognized that most Catholic schools met the unprecedented pandemic situation with courage and resilience, and garnered the public's deeper respect and wider admiration for the quality of education they continued to offer during these crisis years. Peggy G. Carr, commissioner of the National Center for Education Statistics (NCES), notes the following:

> It is clear that the pandemic disruption was a major factor impeding achievement on the 2022 NAEP (National Assessment of Educational Progress) exams for a host of reasons that affected schools, families, and communities. Nationally, we experienced declines between 2019 and 2022 in both mathematics and reading at both grades assessed, grades 4 and 8. But Catholic schools generally fared better than the nation. Catholic schools held steady in all but mathematics at grade 8, where they experienced declines similar to the nation as a whole.[12]

These lessons learned, as well as the development of new financial models to ensure ongoing pandemic-related changes, reflect ideas that now circulate at all levels of education, as there is a strong consensus that education has shifted in a new and somewhat unknown direction. Schools that simply returned to pre-pandemic ways of serving students have missed the opportunity to innovate and reflect an overall failure to grasp the reality that a tectonic shift in education has occurred.

Enterprise Risk Management and Crisis Management

The COVID-19 pandemic and its catastrophic, global impact was an unforeseeable event for the general public and for most

84   *Chapter 4*

educators, save those who work in certain advanced scientific levels in fields such as virology. However, presidents who spent endless hours focused on the very real crisis, with resulting high levels of stress, pressure, and expenditure of energy, also needed to be simultaneously vigilant concerning more foreseeable types of risks and crises, including fires, flooding, security breaches in technology, credible death threats, and active shooter situations—all possible scenarios that require serious preparation. How can presidents be proactive to prepare and prevent these unthinkable situations? How do high-impact leaders anticipate these types of crises?[13]

In 2022 the AGB identified the management of serious risks as one of its top strategic issues, noting the following: "Now more than ever, college and university leaders and their boards must be prepared to deal with a multitude of crises and flashpoints, whether smoldering under the radar or sudden, unexpected conflagrations."[14] A key resource for addressing this top strategic issue is enterprise risk management (ERM), as defined by MacTaggart as "a systematic process for identifying, analyzing and ranking risks in terms of the probability of their occurrence and the severity of impact should they occur."[15] Citing the work of Janice Abraham and other scholars, MacTaggart notes four critical steps involved in ERM: risk identification, risk assessment, risk mitigation planning, and reporting to the board of trustees.[16]

Presidents and boards need to prioritize ERM in their schools, given the stakes concerning cybersecurity, data integrity, and campus security and surveillance protections and the imperative to secure windows and external doors; these are only a few of the many elements involved in promoting a safe school. Most often this process entails hiring a company with ERM experience in educational environments, as these professional companies usually include former law enforcement or fire safety officers.

Comprehensive risk identification and assessment includes recommendations that address practical, immediate needs as

Risk Assessment and Crisis Management 85

well as long-term goals. What are the existing security strengths within the campus? Where are its vulnerabilities? What pressing needs within the community must take priority? Has the school carefully budgeted for the implementation of additional safety measures?

A comprehensive plan that directly results from the ERM process will insist on specific safety protocols for the daily life of the school, including the existence of a representative K-12 safety committee or university public safety office that is charged with monitoring crisis readiness, scheduling regular fire and lockdown drills, verifying the security of various technological firewalls, and assessing the overall physical safety of the campus environment. In addition, the safety committee or public safety office should develop appropriate and prompt emergency alert systems and consistently asks questions in order to ascertain crisis readiness: Do the students, teachers, and staff know the safety protocols expected during fire drills and lockdown exercises? Are safety drills conducted frequently? Are strategies for safety improvement regularly shared as feedback to the community? Are doors that provide exterior access to a building locked at all times, with a protected access system in place for students and employees? Are residence halls protected by restricted access? Are there clear directives for visitor identification and permission to enter a school building? Does the campus have adequate security cameras located throughout the campus, especially at entrances, parking lots, and exits? Of course, leaders must strike a balance between rigorous safety readiness and maintaining a peaceful environment that is conducive to teaching and learning, avoiding an atmosphere where fear dominates.

With multiple administrative demands placed on school leaders, distractions and time pressures can too easily overshadow this paramount focus on safety. ("There are too many things to do; we do not have time for a fire drill.") Complacency can slowly creep into the day-to-day routine. ("It can never happen here.") Unrelenting vigilance must characterize the daily

86 *Chapter 4*

commitment of presidents and senior administrators when it comes to matters related to school safety. It only takes a moment for a fire to erupt, a technology data breach to occur, or an assault to take place, with all the ramifications unleashed by a crisis event, including the critical area of accountability to the wider community.[17]

Part of this proactive stance by presidents includes developing strong relationships with local police, fire, and emergency response officials. By inviting these local community officials to campus to speak periodically to students, faculty, and staff, a president can build the type of safety network that strengthens a school's crisis readiness. In addition to campus presentations, police, fire, and emergency response officials often host safety classes at their local headquarters, where school nurses and other health providers, members of the school's safety committee, administrators, and university public safety officers can learn practical safety steps and establish important relationships.

While no school campus can be 100 percent safe, multiple steps—small and large—can be taken every day to ensure a school has the safest possible environment, with every member of the community—from the youngest student to the most senior employee—exercising responsibility in this critical matter. To the credit of the educational community, most school environments are quite safe, and the academic community can focus on daily teaching and learning experiences in an atmosphere of peace.

The ideas mentioned here are familiar to every educator who has lived through the recent years of the pandemic or who has also been charged with simultaneously maintaining a safe day-to-day school environment in general. Upon reflection regarding these daily risks, as well as the pandemic experience, successful leaders should follow several overarching principles for navigating serious health emergencies and other crises:

1. Develop a deep reservoir of internal strength long before a crisis occurs, as the president must bring the necessary stamina,

Risk Assessment and Crisis Management 87

integrity, clarity, and steadiness required for the role. This is one reason why it is not advisable for educators to assume a presidency too early in their careers when they lack an adequate depth of experience—a depth achieved only through multiple and gradually increasing responsibilities. A crisis is no time to learn on the job. The most successful presidents bring a quality of leadership to the role that reflects extensive experience, unwavering strength, and a natural composure and equanimity.

2. Address crises forthrightly and decisively but with thoughtful care, embracing the moment and exerting great effort to prevent difficult situations from spiraling out of control. Do not flinch nor appear ambivalent in identifying or responding to any moment or situation that risks the safety of the community. It should be clear to the entire community that the president has assumed ultimate responsibility for the school's safety and will do whatever it takes to protect all students and every employee.

3. Demonstrate empathy, concern, and sensitivity for anyone and everyone impacted in a crisis. As the COVID-19 pandemic demonstrated, a range of emotions—uncertainty, fear, anger, loss, dread—can grip a community, and presidential actions and words can bring healing to these difficult situations.

4. Build credibility within the community immediately after assuming the office of president—from day one—then rely on this trust when a crisis occurs, whether the crisis entails threats to the reputation of the school, tensions with the diocese, issues of academic freedom, or a credible death threat. While members of the community may disagree with certain executive decisions, they should have sufficient confidence in their leader to accept these decisions. This dynamic was especially evident during the pandemic, when some teachers, staff, and parents were vocal about their fear of returning to in-person instruction while others were eager to return to campus. It was the task of the president to exhibit compassion and concern while citing

88   *Chapter 4*

all the specific steps that the school had taken to ensure a safe environment. Ultimately, of course, the president must make a decision. While it is unreasonable to assume that 100 percent of the school community will support the decision, one hopes that a "critical mass" will trust their president, confident that the situation is being well-handled.

5. Release frequent and clear communications with content that is thorough; the presentation (in whatever format) must be strong and steady; the tone must reflect sensitivity and understanding. Composure is essential, and no public display of anxiety or anger is appropriate, as these diminish one's credibility. The board of trustees, the president, and all senior administrators need to speak with one voice concerning safety policies and procedures, whether during a multiyear pandemic or concerning the safety restrictions that need to be in place at all times, such as parking bans in emergency vehicle lanes. The goal is to limit public second-guessing or dissension, especially at a time of crisis. Differences of opinion among trustees or administrators need to be addressed behind closed doors, with the final decision stated unambiguously to the community when publicly presented.

6. Possess the humility to constantly seek advice, especially from resources beyond the academic world. Whether in the area of public health, legal obligations, developments in educational technology, risk assessment, or public safety protocols, to cite a few examples, high-impact leaders understand their limitations and constantly look to subject matter experts to keep them informed on best practice strategies and future educational trends. The schools that were best prepared to pivot to all-virtual learning when the pandemic began had scanned the academic best practice environment long before the spring of 2020, making certain financial and pedagogical decisions accordingly. Their advanced, student-centered, 1:1 laptop, flipped classroom methodologies, and teacher/student readiness were well in place

before the pandemic soared into reality. Long before the turmoil and disruption of the pandemic, vigilant schools had also developed the infrastructure and hired the necessary personnel to handle emergencies, such as employing appropriate professionals (for example, school nurses, and public safety officers). Furthermore, high-impact leaders had already forged strategic alliances within the community (police, county health officials, emergency medical services) and did not wait for a crisis to erupt on their campus.

7. Plan a debrief session once a crisis has been resolved in order to process multiple aspects of the crisis. With key trustees and senior members of the leadership team, this session should both study all the dimensions of the specific crisis and the immediate steps that were taken to address it, as well as how the response and recovery process could have been improved. Was the crisis addressed in a timely manner? How long did it take to resolve? Were important resources overlooked? Did the president and other administrators communicate effectively? Many questions should surface during these debrief sessions in order to effectively examine lessons learned and specific steps to improve administrative performance.

Conclusion

To understand the dynamics of aviation, Wilbur Wright observed the flight of manifold birds and took extensive notes to document his findings at Kitty Hawk, North Carolina. After long hours of observation, Wright noted that "no bird soars in a calm."[18] The same could be said for every school president: turbulence (crisis) presents a unique opportunity to demonstrate great character and truly lead a community in a situation that demands strength, resolve, and focus.[19]

Leaders do not get to choose their crises. Traumatic events often come in unexpected ways from unanticipated sources. They test the strength and tenacity of high-impact leaders, and

90 *Chapter 4*

separate them from administrators who flounder at key moments and look to others for direction and answers. "No bird soars in a calm." In truth, communities often forget much of what presidents accomplish during their tenures. Communities never forget, however, how a school's leader handled (or mishandled) a serious crisis.

Assessing Risk and Managing a Crisis

- Understand that the safety of the community is the number one priority.
- Always have a safety plan that is regularly updated and widely distributed throughout the school community.
- Develop a deep reservoir of internal strength. See chapter 6.
- Learn to confront crises forthrightly but with thought and care. Embrace the moment. Do not flinch or appear ambivalent.
- Demonstrate empathy, concern, and sensitivity for all community members directly or indirectly impacted.
- Develop clear, concise communication skills in order to present a strong and steady message.
- Have the humility to seek advice from others, including medical professionals, legal advisors, risk assessment specialists, and emergency responders, to cite a few potential resources. Connect with these community leaders as early as possible when assuming a leadership role.
- Learn to anticipate crises that may impact the security of the school's data systems.
- Understand the importance of "debrief" sessions immediately after, when the event is fresh and the lessons learned are more obvious.

Key Questions

1. Describe your experience within your Catholic school during the COVID-19 pandemic.

Risk Assessment and Crisis Management 91

2. What lessons related to educational quality and school operations did you learn during the most critical pandemic years?

3. Does your school have a representative safety committee? How does this committee function in your school? Have you served on a school's safety committee?

4. Can your school improve its day-to-day safety protocols? If so, how?

5. Does your school have a strong professional relationship with your community's police, fire, and other emergency personnel?

6. How can the school enhance its relationships with government and health safety officials?

7. As a president, have you experienced a safety crisis in your school (other than COVID-19)?

8. As a president, what qualities did you tap to address this safety crisis?

9. Describe and evaluate your own communication skills. What steps would you take to enhance your communications during a crisis?

10. How did you engage your board of trustees during the pandemic? How do you engage your board concerning policies related to everyday safety, especially as these protocols are evaluated by external risk assessment specialists?

Case Study: Risk Assessment and Crisis Management

At 3:10 p.m. on February 6, the dean of students informs you that a handwritten death threat containing a specific date has been found in the corner of a student lounge in a women's residence hall. The note says: "I'll kill people on this campus on February 7." What are the first steps to take? Whom do you inform first? What process do you use to address the situation immediately? Who is on the team you immediately convene? What responsibilities do you immediately delegate? When do you call the police? When do you inform the board of trustees?

92   *Chapter 4*

When and how will you alert the school community without causing widespread panic?

3:14 p.m.: Police arrive on campus to investigate the situation. How do you work effectively with the police in this situation at this time?

3:20 p.m.: You learn that several students who were gathered in the student lounge at 2:55 p.m. had discovered the note and discussed the death threat before informing their residence hall director. Upset by the message, these students also used social media to alert several classmates about the situation. How do you help these particular students? What information do you provide to them at this time? These students did not immediately report the death threat to school authorities. What if any disciplinary action should be taken with these students? How do you address their use of social media in this situation?

3:40 p.m.: A local television network calls your office to confirm a tip concerning the death threat. How do you handle the media in this situation?

4:10 p.m.: At the desperate urging of their friends, two students come forward to disclose their involvement in the "prank." They claim that they are sorry, as they did not realize how much their joke would upset their friends. They did not anticipate the immediate and significant presence of police on campus. How do you confirm the students' version of events? What other immediate steps do you take with these two students?

4:22 p.m.: You have verified that these two students did indeed write the note with no intent to actually harm anyone. Police agree with this assessment. How do you inform the community of this development? Whom else must you contact? What disciplinary action will the two students face? Should any friends who knew about the note also face disciplinary action?

4:45 p.m.: What steps do you take to assess the situation, knowing that a real threat did not exist? How are your actions different from a real threat? Would you have done anything differently? What are the lessons from this situation? How would you improve your response? What education is needed within

Risk Assessment and Crisis Management 93

the community, especially regarding students and their use of social media during a crisis? What moral values were undermined by the situation?

Notes

1. MacTaggart, *Crisis Leadership*, 5.
2. Jon Kemp, "COVID-19 Enters Fourth Year with Serious Illness Waning," *Wall Street Journal*, January 21, 2023. See the CDC's website: https://www.covid.cdc.gov.
3. Blackburn, "COVID Is Here to Stay"; Stephanie Armour and Liz Essley Whyte, "Can We Develop a COVID-19 Vaccine that Lasts?," *Wall Street Journal*, June 17, 2022.
4. McMurtrie, "'A Stunning' Level"; McClure and Fryar, "Great Faculty Disengagement"; Wodon, "COVID-19 Crisis," 13–20; Wodon, *Potential Impact*; Sarah Mervosh, "The Pandemic Erased Two Decades of Progress in Math and Reading," *New York Times*, September 1, 2022; Eric Hanushek, "Finding the Best Teachers for Post-Pandemic Schools," *Wall Street Journal*, August 26, 2022. Since 2020, renaissance.com has released a series of reports titled *How Kids Are Performing,* which have estimated the impact of the COVID-19 pandemic on US student achievement in reading and mathematics; see https:www.renaissance.com/how-kids-are-performing.
5. Concerns about pandemic policies and procedures emanating from the Centers for Disease Control and Prevention and other federal and state official agencies started early and continued throughout the crisis. See, for example, https://www.nejm.org/doi/full/10.1056/nejmp2 006740 https://www.brookings.edu/articles/the-federal-governments -coronavirus-actions-and-failures-timeline-and-themes/ and https://the hill.com/opinion/judiciary/589248-coronavirus-v-government-over reach-which-is-worse/.
6. States varied in the timing of closing and reopening schools, with a range of social, economic, and academic impacts. See "The Coronavirus Spring: The Historic Closing of U.S. Schools (A Timeline)," *Education Week*, July 1, 2020, https://www.edweek.org.
7. Antony et al., *College President Handbook*, 307–8.
8. Dacey, "From Challenge to Opportunity," 18–21; Dallavis, "Fostering Parent Involvement."
9. National Academies of Sciences, Engineering, and Medicine, "Schools Should Prioritize Reopening"; Lauren Camera, "Pediatric Group Calls for Children to Return to Schools Despite Coronavirus," *U.S. News and World Report*, June 29, 2020, https://www.usnews.com

94   *Chapter 4*

/news/education-news/articles/2020-06-29/pediatric-group-calls-for -children-to-return-to-schools-despite-coronavirus.

10. For example, see Travis Andersen, "Boston Archdiocese Schools Are in Session—with a Spike in Students," *Boston Globe,* September 10, 2020. The NCEA notes that Catholic school enrollment grew for two straight years following the resumption of in-person instruction in the fall of 2020, with a proactive approach and strong retention rates as two key factors for the growth. See Snyder, "An Interview."

11. In addition to the pandemic crisis, it is important to acknowledge the intense societal impact of the very public and brutal killing of George Floyd on May 25, 2020. The event directly impacted presidents as they addressed concerns about their schools' curricula and overall support of students of color, often expressed by upset alumni.

12. See Ward and Fassbach, "NAEP 2022 Results for Catholic Schools," webinar for the NCEA, December 15, 2022; Woolhouse, "Catholic Schools Have Stayed (Mostly) Open."

13. See the extensive work of the national nonprofit organization Sandy Hook Promise; Lockdown International, "5 School Safety Measures"; and Temkin et al., "Evolution of State School Safety Laws."

14. AGB, *Top Strategic Issues,* 38.

15. MacTaggart, *Crisis Leadership,* 24.

16. MacTaggart, 23–24; Abraham et al., *Risk Management.*

17. The federal Clery Act (officially the Jeanne Clery Disclosure of Campus Security Policy and Campus Crime Statistics Act) requires colleges and universities in the United States to disclose crime statistics for the campus and surrounding areas. See https://www.clerycenter.org.

18. McCullough, *The Wright Brothers,* 52.

19. See Koehn, *Forged in Crisis.* Koehn's historical analysis of the lives of Ernest Shackleton, Abraham Lincoln, Frederick Douglass, Dietrich Bonhoeffer, and Rachel Carson leads her to conclude that leaders are made, not born.

5

Governance

A SCHOOL CANNOT REALIZE GENUINE, enduring excellence unless strength in governance is deeply rooted and easily apparent. This chapter examines the responsibilities of the board of trustees through the lens of a high-impact leader who promotes an understanding of governance as articulated by Richard P. Chait, William P. Ryan, and Barbara E. Taylor in their work, *Governance as Leadership: Reframing the Work of Nonprofit Boards.*[1] In this context, trustees exercise generative thinking as well as decisive strategic and fiduciary governance, all exceptionally serious obligations that protect the well-being of any school and its future.[2]

Individuals who serve as trustees on nonprofit boards are typically volunteers who selflessly dedicate their time and expertise to improve the school. In Catholic schools they are most often individuals who know and love the school—current parents, past parents, alumni, and members of the community. Frequently they are recruited for their expertise in specific areas: facilities, finance, fundraising, investments, risk assessment, compliance, and other areas pertinent to strategic and fiduciary responsibilities. These individuals generously embrace their responsibilities and deserve the sincere gratitude of the president and the entire school community, as their contribution of "time, talent, and treasure" is immeasurable and influences generations of students.

96   Chapter 5

Critical Issues Facing Boards of Trustees

The unanticipated 2020 jolt of COVID-19 seriously impacted every board of trustees, especially as the pandemic forced most boards to reprioritize their strategic goals. Many unplanned board meetings took place during the pandemic, as trustees met with presidents and senior administrators to determine appropriate policies and procedures for their specific academic communities. In addition, the violent death of George Floyd that same year became a national flashpoint for exposing systemic racism and injustice, topics that became the focus of intense board sessions, especially as many students and alumni voiced deep and often very public concern about their own school's history with racial issues.

While the unanticipated and serious disruptions of the pandemic and the simultaneous civil unrest stretched boards of trustees in new ways, multiple issues remain that can be anticipated and confronted, as identified by the AGB in its *Top Strategic Issues for Boards*: (1) ensuring institutional vitality; (2) improving outcomes for students; (3) strengthening civic education for a functioning democracy; (4) developing new higher education leaders; and (5) managing serious risks.[3]

Catholic schools that are financially healthy can look to reports such as *Top Strategic Issues* as a challenge for them to develop new educational opportunities, including the use of emerging technologies and the creation of enhanced programs for student wellness and other important areas. However, for schools repeatedly failing a basic financial stress test, addressing the most pressing strategic issues can represent a true inflection point and result in serious trustee explorations of structural changes, including institutional mergers, affiliations, partnerships, consolidations, or, as a last resort, closure. In this situation, serious consideration should be given to every option—from remaining an autonomous school to forging a strategic alliance or closing the school—since every option requires significant time and money and the involvement of accrediting agencies, alumni groups, and many other key stakeholders. In all these critical issues facing boards today, it falls to the president and the full board of trustees to assess their school's situation honestly, employing best practices in governance to do so.

While there are excellent comprehensive resources concerning these best practice measures regarding board function, structure, and composition, it is vital to specifically examine how presidents engage trustees in multiple ways on numerous issues, with a focus on interaction with the board chair, executive committee, and governance, finance, and advancement committees.[4] Best practices also include expressions of presidential gratitude for opportunities to work with trustees, recognizing that the chair and all committee members dedicate countless hours to their governance responsibilities. As Richard D. Legon notes, "Voluntary service on governing boards . . . can be highly rewarding. Nonetheless, it requires work and commitment. As boards respond to today's heightened call for appropriate engagement and collaborative leadership, their members must recognize that effective board governance requires constancy, awareness, and curiosity."[5]

Board Chair

While trustees are tasked with multiple responsibilities, one of their most important duties is to attract, hire, and retain talented presidential leadership—and in this very important process the board chair holds the highest level of responsibility for securing the right leader for the school. This responsibility most often includes the selection of a search firm as well as developing an inclusive, collaborative process that secures the insights of employees, students, and alumni. This task is made more challenging by the generational leadership shift occurring in Catholic education today, as a wave of presidential retirements, planned or prompted by the pandemic, takes place.[6]

98   *Chapter 5*

Regarding the selection of a president—from candidacy, through the hiring process, and beyond—the following areas are critical throughout the process:

1. While a candidate may bring strong academic credentials to the role, as well as significant experience in areas such as planning, finance, and fundraising, an essential priority centers on evaluating the candidate's understanding of and appreciation for the Catholic mission of the school, the "mission fit" of the candidate. It is incumbent on the board chair, the search committee, and ultimately the entire board of trustees to challenge candidates concerning their belief in the school's Catholic mission and their readiness to promote that mission untiringly. To assure this level of mission commitment, many Catholic schools require that the presidential office be held by a practicing Catholic.[7]

2. Candidates must exhibit an ability to interact with the board chair with mutual respect and trust, as this will be a key relationship for the president during his or her tenure. All other hiring conversations that follow—regarding the description of the position, performance expectations, compensation, and evaluation processes—build on the fundamental understanding that the president and the board share a common goal: to serve the school with integrity.

3. Candidates should also demonstrate a willingness to seek advice from the board chair, even in early encounters during the hiring process. It should be assumed that the board chair knows the school community and its culture and will provide important information about the "climate" of the school and other insights that are not readily available on the school's website or in the search materials. Mutual trust should be the centerpiece of this working relationship.

4. Once hired, the president must have confidence in the unambiguous support from the board chair, a commitment

Governance   99

demonstrated at all times when interacting with the full board and throughout the entire school community. When missing, if only on one occasion, significant tensions and problems arise, as leadership credibility and authority can be immediately weakened and decisions undermined, with the potential effect of impeding the smooth functioning of the school as well as any real attempt to plan the future. Tensions, serious conflicts, or competition between the board chair and the president must be addressed immediately, and failure to do so does not bode well, especially for the president's success.

5. Strong support from the board chair should be reflected in the quality of the onboarding process, which the board chair should design specifically for the new president, as the first few months of a new leader's tenure are significant in establishing a solid foundation on which subsequent months and years will build. In addition to introductory meetings with key school committees (alumni board, student council officers, executive committee of the parents' association, etc.), the onboarding process usually includes one-on-one meetings between each trustee and the new president, during which they can discuss a wide array of the trustee's priorities, concerns, and expectations. In these meetings presidents can listen carefully to garner invaluable insights about how trustees understand their role and identify their top priorities for the school. In future months and years, the successful president will develop these relationships by taking the time to get to know the trustees outside regularly scheduled committee or full board meetings. Trustees appreciate a leader who seeks their advice and who genuinely values the service they render.

6. Throughout the hiring and onboarding process and beyond, the board chair and president ideally develop an ongoing professional relationship characterized by trust, honest communication, and the ability to disagree (in confidence). In addition to establishing a mutual willingness to dedicate substantial hours

100   *Chapter 5*

to executive planning, the president and board chair agree that very serious situations are jointly addressed with a sense of immediacy. These issues can range from a high-profile personnel disciplinary situation to a social media posting that threatens the reputation of the school. As is the case with most presidents, board chairs do not like surprises. When fully informed concerning a particularly sensitive issue, the chair can offer invaluable assistance to the president in areas such as communication processes or engagement of legal counsel.

7. When the relationship between the board chair and president is functioning well, they can realize one of their top priorities: guiding the board to a strategic form of governance (versus the easy tendency for trustees to become entangled in the managerial level). In order to work well, boards need to function at the 40,000-foot level of oversight, versus the temptation to function at 10,000-foot level and mistakenly immerse themselves in the organization's daily operations.[8] If trustees are spending time debating parking problems or cafeteria supply issues, the type of strategic thinking that truly reimagines a school's future cannot take place. Likewise, staying at the strategic level reminds board chairs that they should not micromanage the president.

8. Boards also need to function in a high-impact manner, with the broad chair and president ultimately setting the agenda and pace of innovation, thereby offsetting any tendencies toward complacency within a board culture or flat, *pro forma* trustee engagement.

Executive Committee

The executive committee, composed of the trustees selected to lead the various board committees, the board vice chair, and the board chair (who presides), is a key additional resource and sounding board for presidents.[9] One of this committee's greatest services is to vet presidential ideas and plans rigorously prior

Governance 101

to their presentation to the full board for approval. These decisions can range from approval of the school's annual operating budget to major investment policies for the school's portfolio. Conducting an initial and thorough executive committee review of all forthcoming presidential recommendations hones the leader's ability to advocate successfully for the many significant matters that must come to the full board for approval, such as an increase in employee salaries or the selection of a new enterprise software system, to cite two examples. The executive committee appropriately asks: Does this recommendation fit the school's Catholic mission? What is the rationale for proceeding with this recommendation, and where is the supporting data, including quantified community input? How does the cost/benefit analysis support this recommendation? Which budget line does this recommendation directly impact?

Pressuring leaders to defend their recommendations with supporting data and predicted financial implications ultimately strengthens the proposal, as it forces crispness of thought, an ability to distill key ideas, and clarity of expression. The process also helps the president anticipate objections to the presentation when offered to the full board, as trustees who serve on the executive committee know the pulse of their committee membership and have experience within the broader school culture (students, parents, alumni). For these reasons, trustees on the executive committee offer extraordinary help with process and communication when they test the strength of presidential recommendations and their rationales, the thoroughness of the data, and other supporting information. This process also assists presidents in anticipating questions and objections at the full board level and ultimately sharpens a president's thinking and communication.

Most especially, the executive committee is an invaluable resource in a crisis, as the president and the executive committee together "think out" all the ramifications of a particular issue (for example, the sudden and immense impact of COVID-19 or a serious personnel matter that potentially affects the school's

102   *Chapter 5*

reputation). The wise president relies on the committee's counsel throughout the academic year, and the result is better preparation for full board meetings and avoidance of serious missteps or setbacks.

Governance Committee

From the perspective of the president, several areas of collaboration with the governance committee should take priority. The first area centers on the development of a clear and concise school-based board of trustees' handbook that contains the board's mission statement, a brief history of the school, a list of committee members for the academic year, dates and times for all scheduled committee and full board meetings, trustee best practice principles, essential committee functions, and other specific expectations stipulated in the school's charter and other legal documents.[10] This handbook, updated annually and distributed to every trustee prior to the beginning of the academic year, serves as a critical guide for trustees and school leaders, as it delineates clear processes, procedures, and areas of responsibility.

A trustee handbook also enables the board to hold itself accountable on all governance matters, especially its functioning, by articulating its annual goals as well as committee-specific subgoals, against which all trustees can measure progress at the end of the academic year. In addition, this document addresses conflict-of-interest issues, stresses the importance of trustee attendance at meetings and engagement as a whole, promotes participation in professional development opportunities, and confirms the requirement for a systematic self-evaluation process in order to improve board performance and service to the school.

The second priority for the governance committee that directly impacts the president focuses on the critical need for confidentiality in all trustee deliberations, either at the committee or full board levels. This is one reason why many boards use the secure environment of a password-protected board portal in order to share key documents and all other trustee materials. By clearly stating the importance of confidentiality as a key principle, the actions of the governance committee directly support overall board integrity. Honest debate and discernment can take place only in an environment of trust, with the knowledge that one's position or the outcome of a particular vote will not become public and potentially risk great harm to the school community. This breach can impact the reputation of an individual trustee, the president, or the board as a whole. When confidentiality is violated, it is incumbent on the board chair and governance committee to intervene and address the situation; this responsibility is only heightened when an individual trustee has "gone rogue" by publicly or frequently denouncing the president's actions (often concerning personnel decisions) or decisions of the entire board (frequently on financial matters). For the overall well-being of a school community, in these cases swift action by the board chair and governance committee is necessary; in rare cases, intervention can result in the removal of the trustee from the board. Likewise, if the president engages in misconduct or commits a serious breach of confidentiality or general dereliction of duty, the board chair and governance committee must address the matter forthrightly and immediately.

An additional key responsibility within the governance committee and the president centers on succession planning for all board committees, especially given the importance of maintaining gender balance and racial and ethnic diversity. Many schools find it advisable that trustees have term limits (for example, three-year terms, with possible renewal for an additional three years), that enable the board to incorporate new talent and fresh perspectives on a regular basis while keeping the size of the board manageable. Governance committees, however, are challenged with balancing these trustee transitions by maintaining strong ties with highly effective trustees who have dedicated years of successful service to the school. In an effort to sustain

104   *Chapter 5*

a trustee's high level of talent and engagement, a governance committee will often recommend *emeritus* or *emerita* status for long-serving individuals.

Often the school's institutional advancement office (an umbrella office that typically includes the offices of admissions, communications, and development) plays a significant role in the task of succession planning. By definition this office has direct contact with all incoming students and their parents, oversees the alumni office, identifies potential donors using wealth analysis tools, and interacts with the broader community through its marketing efforts. Relying on this vital information, the president and chair of the governance committee are able to identify strong candidates for trusteeship. These individuals can be vetted by assigning them for one or two years to a board committee that permits nontrustee membership (for example, the investment committee) prior to a formal invitation to trusteeship by a vote of the full board. In this way the governance committee can assess commitment, engagement, expertise, and genuine interest on the part of an individual before offering a formal recommendation to the full board of trustees.

Careful succession planning is essential to maintaining a strong, strategic board and this ongoing process of gaining new members throughout the academic year cannot be neglected due to time pressures or other distractions. High-impact leaders understand its importance and identify this process among their top priorities.

Finance Committee

Given the disruption in Catholic education today, the critical strategic and fiduciary role of the board of trustees has heightened the role of the finance committee in recent years. Working closely with the president and the school's chief financial officer, this committee develops policies and procedures, monitors the five-year financial planning model, oversees the annual budget (including quarterly income and cash flow statements), examines capital budget expenditures, studies the annual audit as submitted by a certified auditing firm, and works with the school's external investment firm, to cite just a few of the committee's responsibilities. Presidents should expect intense interactions with this committee and welcome the critical analysis and debate concerning a wide range of important financial proposals, including annual budget recommendations and compensation projections.

Given the current shift in the entire field of education, however, a finance committee must also transcend general operational decisions within any given fiscal year and look broadly at the dramatic impact of various trends or events (such as the pandemic) along with recent demographic trends and economic developments. This is especially the case when a Catholic school struggles to maintain healthy enrollments and stable finances. When faced with a harsh situation that bears the "generative landmarks" described by Chait, Ryan, and Taylor—ambiguity, saliency, high stakes, serious strife, and the irreversibility of certain decisions—the president should encourage trustees to frame the moment as a "what-if" opportunity to consider alternative educational models, which might include institutional mergers, affiliations, consolidations, or partnerships or may even extend to community-based organizations or the corporate world.[11] While the entire board is clearly involved in such serious decisions, the president and financial committee can serve as the catalyst for an assessment process by demonstrating the courage to reimagine the school's current organizational structure and ultimate future.

Advancement Committee

Successful Catholic communities place the school's mission at the center of all advancement efforts to promote the school's core values by strengthening its financial situation. How does this gift help the school fulfill its mission? How does donor generosity impact the quality of the student's experience? How can

106   *Chapter 5*

this gift enhance the professional development opportunities for the teachers and staff? How will a generous philanthropic offering provide new educational facilities? The board's advancement committee must position all fundraising efforts within these relational contexts and articulate clearly that generous giving to Catholic schools significantly impacts the fulfillment of the school's mission and the quality of the education offered.

The advancement committee should also help trustees recognize the school as one of their top three philanthropic priorities. By achieving 100 percent trustee giving to the school's annual fund, the board assures the academic community and the public (including foundations) that the trustees are leading the way in philanthropic efforts. Other responsibilities of the advancement committee include hosting donor recognition events and sessions to educate the entire regional or national community concerning the value of a Catholic education and the importance of obtaining generous financial gifts to support these values, including planned giving and grants from private foundations.

The more complex aspect of philanthropic work is the successful planning and execution of a comprehensive campaign, since it raises both operational and capital funds.[12] When carefully aligned with the school's strategic planning process, the board-appointed campaign committee works directly with the president to map a five- or six-year process by which campaign goals can be realized, including a clear and sophisticated strategy that includes projecting the schedule for both the quiet and public phases of the comprehensive campaign. Again, the school's advancement office provides invaluable assistance in this process, using the office's tools for wealth analysis and other background information to carefully establish potential donors (analysis of the donor's interests, past giving history, and so forth).

From the high-impact president's perspective, certain key fundraising principles help immensely at the beginning of and throughout an entire comprehensive campaign:

Governance   107

1. Situate the school's mission and strategic plan as the foundation of the campaign. It signals the seriousness of the undertaking and the mission's essential role in realizing carefully identified community-based goals. The president must clearly demonstrate how the campaign funds will directly impact students and help them achieve their hopes and dreams. Parents and the wider school community will find inspiration in a campaign that incorporates these substantive matters at its very core.

2. Do not hesitate to advocate for a bold stretch goal for the overall campaign. Too often Catholic school communities underestimate what they can actually achieve. Too often campaigns set the bar too low, simply to assure success. While external professional consultants can assist with measuring a community's capacity for fundraising, the president should also caution the community not to underestimate itself and its ability to raise significant amounts of support.

3. Be prepared to spend extended professional time on a comprehensive campaign. The initial phase of building relationships and introducing a campaign to the school community takes many meetings in varied formats, including informal gatherings with parents and alumni as well as one-on-one sessions with potential donors—all of which should be focused on the campaign and specific donor interest. For example, interactions with parents is important in any K-12 independent school, as this group usually comprises the highest percentage of campaign donors, while in a diocesan setting, interactions with foundations and corporate organizations merits special attention. In colleges and universities, alumni giving often constitutes the strongest source of philanthropy, and therefore strong ties throughout the alumni community are essential for achieving campaign success in higher education. These many campaign commitments will usually involve extensive travel, long hours, multiple meetings, and the president's strong reliance on the senior leadership team

108 *Chapter 5*

to manage the school's day-to-day demands. However, certain school events require a president's participation (e.g., ceremonies at the start of the academic year, special holiday celebrations, alumni weekends, graduation). Nevertheless, the demands of a comprehensive campaign do not stop but rather add another significant layer of responsibility throughout the academic year. In this way, leading a comprehensive campaign is a fundraising marathon, requiring energy, stamina, and commitment to an intense, multiyear effort in the service of the school.

4. Allocate the time and preparation for meetings with significant donors who have the capacity to make truly transformational gifts to the campaign. What constitutes a "transformational" gift differs from school to school, but the principle is the same: campaigns cannot achieve success without very generous gifts from key donors, as approximately 80 percent of all money raised usually comes from approximately 20 percent of all donors. Stanley Weinstein and Pamela Barden's work on fundraising management notes that the 80/20 rule is becoming the 90/10 rule in many capital campaigns and mature fundraising programs.[13] It is, therefore, essential for campaign success that the president spend significant time with these relatively few individuals, understanding their relationship to the school, appreciating their specific philanthropic interests, and cultivating their commitment to support top priorities within the campaign.

5. Do not hesitate to ask for generous gifts from all parents, past parents, alumni members, and others who have special ties to the school, once the community is aware of the importance of the campaign, usually during its public phase. Potential donors are often asked why they did not contribute to the school's fundraising efforts, only to respond that no one asked them for a gift. Members of the community expect a school's leaders and trustees to make "the ask," and individuals respond most often with gracious generosity when a relationship of trust has been thoughtfully established.

Governance 109

6. Make the right connections. Most trustees who serve on Catholic school boards are intimately connected with the philanthropic and corporate community and have the ability to introduce presidents to certain foundation heads and corporate sponsors who are likely to support the school's fundraising efforts. These vital resources are critical to securing support from resources beyond the immediate school community; such support also enhances the public reputation of the academic community, as accrediting bodies assess fundraising success as part of their overall evaluation of the school. If the school does not have a designated person to oversee the management of grants, it should be outsourced to professionals who specialize in this area.

7. Establish regional alumni advisory councils. These councils should meet at least once a year in a well-planned session, during which the president reviews the school's strategic plan, the campus master plan, innovative curricular programs, and enrollment data, with a request for feedback on how the school's current programs align with corporate workplace needs. Informed council members serve as ambassadors to their former classmates in promoting regional meetings and participation in professional affinity groups and career networking opportunities. They also encourage the financial support of the alma mater by reminding others of its distinguished faculty, dedicated staff, and current students.

8. Cultivate a culture of giving and gratitude. Simple handwritten notes, a special phone call, a breakfast or luncheon invitation—there are many thoughtful ways to acknowledge a gift and express the heartfelt gratitude of the community. A positive approach usually results in building strong relationships with donors that extends far beyond the campaign and is much more effective than the "we need money" approach.

9. Carefully consider all gift offers and every donor's intent. It has been said that "no gift is too small, no gift too large";

110   *Chapter 5*

however, it is incumbent upon the president and the advancement committee to vet the offer of gifts carefully in order to ensure that the intent of the donor genuinely matches the priorities of the school. Donors sometimes need to be (gently) redirected to make a gift that reflects a priority identified in the campaign. They may need encouragement to reimagine their gift's potential vis-à-vis the school's strategic goals. If handled properly, donors can come to see fresh possibilities for their gifts and can take pride in their contributions to realizing specific campaign goals.

10. Appreciate that philanthropic work is a privilege. During a campaign, trustees and presidents often meet with thousands of people. In these interactions, donors may openly and confidentially share very personal stories about themselves and their families—from moments of great joy to times of difficult loss. While raising money is important for the future of the school, especially during a campaign, more important are all the conversations that gradually establish an enduring relationship of trust, a gift more precious than any dollar raised or specific campaign goal achieved.

Conclusion

This chapter has emphasized some central issues facing presidents and their work with Catholic school boards, as well as the very unique and important responsibilities assumed by the board chair and executive, governance, finance, and advancement committees. To explore all comprehensive aspects of trusteeship, including assessment of members' qualifications, plans for recruitment, the design of the onboarding and orientation process, support of professional development, and ongoing evaluation—and other areas concerning board composition and structure—consult the comprehensive materials produced by the NCEA, the ACCU, the AGB, and the National Association of Independent Schools (NAIS).[14]

How Does a President Collaborate Successfully with a Board of Trustees?

- Never take for granted the service of trustees. At all times show deep respect and appreciation for the dedicated time, talent, and treasure that trustees offer to the school.
- Make every effort to develop a strong working relationship with the board chair that is marked by mutual respect, trust, understanding, and honesty.
- Always keep the board chair informed of important developments within the school.
- Get to know all the trustees, especially members of the executive committee.
- Invite the executive committee to challenge and rigorously examine all presidential recommendations prior to meetings of the full board.
- Seek the counsel of all trustees, both in committee meetings but also in less formal sessions during which you learn about their broader interests.
- Develop a comprehensive trustee handbook in coordination with the governance committee in order to clarify the board structure and the roles, responsibilities, processes, and expectations of trustees.
- Expect a marathon when launching a comprehensive campaign. For this reason, the planning phase of a campaign must be carefully executed.
- Always position the school's mission as the foundation for the campaign; structure the campaign itself around the goals identified in the school's strategic plan.
- Cherish the enduring relationships that you establish during a campaign.

Key Questions

1. As president, describe your relationship with your board chair.

112   *Chapter 5*

2. As president, describe your relationship with the board of trustees as a whole.

3. How frequently does your executive committee meet? Does this committee plan the agendas for full board meetings?

4. Do the board committees establish annual goals that are shared with the full board and assessed at the end of the academic year?

5. Does the board of trustees have a trustee handbook? If so, how is it used by the trustees? Are there additional components that should be included in the handbook's next edition?

6. Does the governance committee understand that succession planning is one of its top goals? If so, how does this process of recruitment function?

7. Have you participated in the planning of a comprehensive campaign?

8. If yes, how frequently did you meet with the campaign chairs? Did your school use an external consultant to assess campaign readiness? What time frame did you devote to the completion of the campaign?

9. Have you been involved in seeking grants from foundations and corporate organizations?

10. Do you have experience working with donors? How did you cultivate a genuine relationship with all donors? How did you express gratitude for their generosity?

Case Study: Governance

The Miller family has been involved with your school for generations, and the entire family proudly attends alumni events every year. Roberta (Crane) Miller, class of '86, graduated in the top ten of her class as a highly respected student government president and award-winning mathematics team member. After graduating she earned great financial success with her software engineering company and is now one of the school's top donors. On campus the newly opened Miller Engineering Center features state-of-the-art classroom facilities and a central social

Governance 113

hub that opens onto stations for design innovation, biotechnology, advanced imaging, computer engineering, information science, and nanotechnology. Recently the school's board of trustees voted to appoint Mrs. Miller as a new trustee, with the request that she serve on the board's advancement committee.

Mrs. Miller is very proud to see her daughter, Amanda, flourishing at her alma mater. Amanda is president of the National Honor Society, a member of the student government senior leadership team, and captain of the robotics team. The family legacy of leadership continues.

Mrs. Miller has just seen Amanda's summer reading list and is very upset to see certain books listed; a few are focused on topics that she believes to be highly inappropriate for a Catholic school. She has just called your office and requested an immediate appointment. Roberta follows up on her call with an email to you, which states that she also wants the chair of the board of trustees to join in the meeting, given the seriousness of the situation. She states that she is now reconsidering her acceptance of an appointment to the board and a donation to fund several STEM scholarships beginning next year.

How do you handle the situation? Whom should you consult first? Do you meet with Mrs. Miller immediately? Do you agree that the board chair should attend the meeting? Should you contact the English Department chair—who created the list—and request that the books be immediately withdrawn from the reading list?

List the steps (in chronological order) that you need to take to resolve this situation.

Notes

1. Chait, Ryan, and Taylor, *Governance as Leadership*.
2. The president usually holds an ex officio position on the board of trustees.
3. AGB, *Top Strategic Issues*.
4. NCEA, *National Standards,* 17–19; ACCU, "Trustees" program; Orem and Wilson, *Trustee Handbook*; NAIS, *Trendbook 2022–23;* AGB, *Higher Education Governing Boards*.

114　*Chapter 5*

5. Richard D. Legon, quoted in foreword of AGB, *Higher Education Governing Boards,* iii.
6. For an assessment of leadership turnover and succession in higher education in general, see AGB, *Top Strategic Issues,* 31–35.
7. For important dimensions concerning this requirement on the K-12 level, see Regan, *Reflections on Catholic School Leadership.*
8. Chait, Ryan, and Taylor, *Governance as Leadership,* 163–82.
9. Like the president, the board chair serves on all board committees.
10. Orem and Wilson, *Trustee Handbook.*
11. Chait, Ryan, and Taylor, *Governance as Leadership,* 107.
12. NCEA, *National Standards,* 27–32; Weinstein and Barden, *Complete Guide,* 225–52. See also the websites of the Council for the Advancement and Support of Education (https://www.case.org) and the *Chronicle of Philanthropy* (https://www.philanthropy.com).
13. Weinstein and Barden, *Complete Guide,* 4–5.
14. See the websites of the NCEA (https://ncea.org), the ACCU (https://www.accunet.org), the AGB (https://agb.org/), and the NAIS (https://www.nais.org).

6

Qualities of High-Impact Leadership

THE PREVIOUS CHAPTERS PRESENTED some of the serious responsibilities and key functions required of a president. This chapter explores the qualities that characterize a successful high-impact leader who can achieve numerous strategic goals developed within a very concise time frame—goals that realize immediate and long-term transformational effects on the educational organization. This model of leadership embraces a robust pace but also uses a highly collaborative, community-based model of planning in which all constituents are invited and encouraged to participate.

How does one become a high-impact leader? What types of experience and expertise are needed for such leadership? While an effective president can display any one of various personality styles (introvert, extravert, reserved, or flamboyant), there are numerous qualities that are advocated in important works on leadership.[1] Some qualities are especially relevant to the style of education leadership advocated here.

Clarification: Leadership Is Not the Same as Management

Is leadership the same as management? The short answer to this question is "no." While all administrators are managers in that

116   *Chapter 6*

they oversee staff and budgets and assure the day-to-day smooth functioning of a school, not all managers have the time, talent, ability, or even desire to lead, especially at a senior level. By definition, managers appreciate and deeply understand the various operational components that make up their departments (academics, admissions, facilities, finance, information resources, marketing communications, and student life). Genuine leadership, however, requires much more, as the effective leader must develop a mindset that demonstrates multiple qualities, including a "both-and" perspective, or the practice of balancing the immediate needs of day-to-day school operations with implications of the future functions, interactions, and possibilities between and among the various departments and constituencies of the school as a whole.

Qualities of High-Impact Leadership

Both-And Creative Tension

To constantly exercise both-and thinking, the president must master the art of holding immediate moments and multiple dimensions of the academic community in creative tension: simultaneously balancing the strategic and the tactical, theory and practice, immediate versus long-term, formulation and implementation, and the needs of the entire community versus individual requests.

This both-and quality enables leaders to be comfortable with multiple dimensions of any given group or question—while clearly seeing the present, they must also constantly think ahead. Effective leaders do not allow themselves to become so swamped with daily operational issues that they have no time to think broadly, theoretically, or strategically. They also do not accept easy or superficial solutions to a problem, that is, a "quick fix" decision executed without thought or analysis of long-term consequences or impact on the school community.

True leaders never stop asking questions: Is restructuring

Qualities of High-Impact Leadership 117

necessary in order to achieve more efficiency and enduring fiscal stability? Is the school data accurate and seamless in its functioning? Is the organization adhering to its five-year financial plan? What are the long-term consequences of reshaping enrollment vis-à-vis the school's current facilities and infrastructure? Do the teachers and the staff have adequate professional development resources? What would be the wider impact of adding a new athletic program? Do current student wellness programs meet the needs of all students?

It is ultimately the responsibility of the president to ensure that this creative tension also constitutes the worldview held by the senior leadership team, even as these administrators manage their day-to-day responsibilities. Presidents need to call their senior leaders to transcend daily management issues, important though they may be. Over time this executive-level vigilance helps develop a certain mindset and outlook within the community as a whole, which gradually comes to see itself more strategically. At some level this both-and approach becomes part of the school culture, thus facilitating community-wide processes such as the renewal of accreditation or an enterprise system migration. With vigilant both-and thinking and frequent communication by administrators, the community becomes familiar with this type of creative tension and is less fearful of moving beyond the status quo.

Exercising continual both-and thinking is hard work and takes great energy. It requires command of both the facts and implications of any serious decision with study and significant "think time" exerted in order to understand strategy and tactics, educational trends, and best practices, as well as the meaning of financial reports, enrollment data, and other gathered information. With this type of thorough preparation, presidents can approach board meetings and community gatherings ready to present the current school situation in a clear, confident manner. They are thus able to articulate concrete ways by which the school can achieve higher levels of excellence in the future marked by fiscal accountability and minimum risk.

118   *Chapter 6*

The Importance of Plan B

While high-impact leaders always balance the both-and, they are also vigilant about the importance of generating a "Plan B" for important matters, that is, a backup strategy or way of proceeding that is readily available should the chosen plan fail.[2] This type of mindset anticipates the possibility of the initial plan's failure (the what-if) and is willing to dedicate an additional layer of time, energy, and thought to generate a second route to success. This planning approach yields significant dividends should Plan A go awry, especially when there is little time to shape another backup strategy, as in the middle of a crisis. Developing this ability to consider alternatives and cultivating this type of thinking within the senior leadership team will allow the school to avoid a range of problems, from inconveniences to mishaps or embarrassments to wrong decisions that directly affect the school's reputation.

Integrity and Honesty

Journalist Peggy Noonan notes that good leaders have many qualities, one of which is the ability to "shift strategies and tactics but not principles."[3] Put another way: strong leaders have integrity and authenticity. Their faculty, staff, and students trust them to make good decisions, even if they do not always agree with their decisions. Successful presidents command respect, even when their decisions are unpopular. The school community should see a leader who is honest and genuine and acts without "smoke screen" or "gaslighting" maneuvers or other distractions that eventually cause the community to lose confidence in the leader and the leader's message. High-impact leaders say what they mean and believe in what they say. Transparent and accountable, they always demonstrate integrity and authenticity, thereby instilling both stability and confidence throughout the community.

Qualities of High-Impact Leadership   119

Innovation

A brief word on innovation is appropriate here. High-impact leaders are innovative by nature. They are not afraid of the new, different, or unfamiliar, but rather see the field of education, which constantly examines theories and pushes intellectual boundaries, as the best frontier for new possibilities. While high-impact leaders are grounded in reality, they also have the ability to see new patterns and arrangements within reality itself; they embrace ambiguity even as they carefully develop new ways to test ideas and explore new organizational structures. They take risks without being reckless; they seek excellence but not elitism; they prefer simple approaches but reject simplistic and superficial solutions. This type of leadership does not hesitate to ask disruptive questions such as "What if?" and "Why not?"

Regarding innovation, high-impact presidents should take the time to study individuals who are widely recognized for their groundbreaking work: women and men who achieved international acclaim by using their creativity, drive, persistence, and success to enable the world to see itself in a new way.[4]

Decisiveness

Psychologist Constance Dierickx notes that effective leaders are firm, clear, and decisive about their goals and decisions, even as they are flexible concerning how to implement those goals and decisions.[5] Catholic school leaders make decisions every day, some of which have serious ramifications with significant financial implications and long-term consequences for the school community. While boards of trustees, a sponsoring religious community, or the bishop may have ultimate authority for significant decisions (depending on the governance structure), all these groups should be able to respect and rely on presidential recommendations, as there is an assumption that the leader has

120   *Chapter 6*

weighed multiple aspects of a proposal, including risks and rewards, as well as a thorough cost-benefits analysis.

In addition to these calculations, a successful leader is also able to articulate to the school's board why a particular decision aligns with the school's Catholic mission and is also the right way forward for the academic community. Trustees appreciate a leader who offers a request or recommendation respectfully but resolutely, as nothing frustrates board members more than an indecisive president. While the board has the authority to modify or reject a presidential request or recommendation, trustees expect and genuinely appreciate clarity and direction from the president.

However, a cautionary note is in order, as there are many steps that are usually taken prior to arriving at a decision. Did the leader utilize a thorough process to reach this particular decision? For instance, did the president use a collaborative model of consultation and communication? Depending on the issue, this collaboration may have taken place with the entire community or may be restricted to the senior leadership team. In some cases this consultation only occurs among the president and board members (most often the executive committee). Effective leaders also should resist the temptation to be wedded to their own ideas. Tenacity is laudable; stubbornness is not. Have they examined whether or not this decision reflects a certain blindness on their part?[6] Have they sufficiently challenged their own ideas and assumptions? Answering these honest questions tests the validity and authenticity of every decision.

While school administrators make many day-to-day decisions, there are always some very serious decisions, often involving the hiring or termination of an employee or the suspension or dismissal of a student. In every case, the exercise of due diligence and the practice of justice are essential, and the values of integrity and fairness must be upheld at all times. It is not unusual to hear a president claim that employee terminations or student dismissals are the toughest decisions within the president's scope of responsibility. Such cases require significant

Qualities of High-Impact Leadership 121

time and energy and a high degree of prayerful discernment. In addition, a certain loneliness comes with making these kinds of decisions, as leaders cannot discuss or disclose their rationale or the particulars of any case (or with very few people, on a "need to know" basis, i.e., the board chair or the executive committee of the board of trustees).

In the end, high-impact leaders who trust their judgment and believe in their decisions are able to defend them and accept their consequences. With the satisfaction that they have kept the safety and well-being of all members of the school community as their top priority, they can rest in a certain peace with their decisions, knowing that they have given their best effort in every serious situation.

Communication

While every high-impact leader need not have the gift of eloquence, all must have the ability to communicate confidently, clearly, concisely, and frequently to the many and varied constituencies within the school community. By keeping their communications centered on the core mission and rooted in accurate facts, the leader is able to deliver a focused message without resorting to conjecture, assumption, or educational jargon. Additionally, the high-impact leader masters the ability to tailor the same content to all groups with whom they specifically interact. What type of message resonates best with parents or alumni and their daily worlds? What is the best way to connect with the faculty and staff? What makes sense to students? How does one communicate with external constituencies, such as officials from the diocese in which the school is situated or regional media and national professional organizations?

The content of communications varies, of course, but so too must the tone and delivery. At times the president needs to exhibit empathy, as was done consistently throughout the pandemic crisis years. On other occasions a celebratory tone is appropriate. The best speakers have an intuitive sense of the

122   *Chapter 6*

importance of the specific communication and the mood of the audience. They "read" the moment and adjust accordingly, without deviating from their central message. For this reason, a leader needs to be comfortable speaking extemporaneously if the moment calls for this type of pivot.

Most successful presidents are teachers at heart, and the most outstanding leaders are great teachers.[7] Strong leaders never take their authority for granted, as they appreciate the power of their words and understand that their sphere of influence extends well beyond what they experienced during their early days of teaching in a traditional classroom. Like any great teacher, a high-impact president understands complexity but also has the ability to simplify by mastering the art of clear, concise communication (and the role of appropriate humor). Like any great teacher, a successful leader is able to prioritize and distill the ideas and information that are the most significant points at any given moment.

Senior leaders, especially the president, are public figures within the school community who appreciate the importance of addressing large audiences as well as extending a simple greeting to everyone within the community, regardless of their role in the school. These one-on-one encounters happen throughout the school day—in a school corridor or cafeteria—and a simple "hello" from the school's leader can mean a great deal. While it may be difficult to know the names of all the employees and students, depending on the size of the school, a warm greeting reflects both recognition of and respect for the other's dignity and important contribution to the community and cultivates the type of cordial environment that all Catholic schools should attempt to foster.

While availability for informal encounters is important, presidents should frequently conduct scheduled dialogues throughout the academic year for all the constituencies of the school community, as they can learn a great deal from these meetings and learn the true "pulse" of the campus. Examples of structured dialogues include periodic town hall meetings with students, alumni receptions, early morning meetings with

Qualities of High-Impact Leadership 123

teachers and staff, or an open forum for parents and guardians. There are unlimited possibilities for the structure, but the important point is that these sessions are carefully promulgated concerning their purpose and are scheduled at a time for optimal participation. Participants should be assured that the meeting reflects an open atmosphere and the opportunity to express concerns and questions in an honest manner.

Perhaps no event tests the ability to communicate more than the death of a faculty or staff member or, even more so, the death of a student. This loss heavily impacts classmates, teachers, and the entire school community. What words bring healing at such a time? How does a president demonstrate compassion, sensitivity, kindness, and understanding at these moments? How does the Catholic community bring this loss to prayer and liturgical ceremonies? What strength can the Catholic community provide to console the family immediately impacted by this death? These very difficult moments challenge leaders to meet such great loss with deep empathy and a quiet and steady presence.

Presidents recognize that they can always improve their communication skills. As with other qualities of leadership, educational leaders study great speeches that addressed certain serious political or societal moments with courage and insight.[8] What made this particular leader an extraordinary speaker? What is the content, tone, and length of the speech? What motivated this speech? How did you feel as you read or listened to this speech? Great speeches can provoke questions that assist a leader in their never-ending quest for improvement, a goal that ultimately strengthens the school community as well.

Time Management

One time-tested means to maintaining professional balance is to carefully manage the daily, weekly, and yearly calendar, as precious minutes can and do slip away. Pace and availability are important, and a carefully maintained calendar is a major means of protecting leaders from persons or departments that

124   *Chapter 6*

seek to absorb time disproportionately. An imbalanced schedule results in the neglect of crucial duties that presidents alone can fulfill. Furthermore, the successful president cannot afford to procrastinate, as the work does not stop and will eventually overwhelm any leader who is unable to prioritize carefully and address important matters in a timely manner.

Appointments, presentations, business travel, receptions, board meetings—these all require careful scheduling in order to yield productive sessions that start punctually and end on time, and especially with anticipated outcomes achieved. For this reason, the successful leader should always seek to hire an administrative assistant who can serve as an effective "gatekeeper." This assistant should be able to sense the most pressing issues versus matters that can be addressed later. She or he does not isolate the president from the school community but is able to balance the intense demands placed upon the president and ensure the time needed to prepare for meetings, to write, to read, and to rest and relax.

Despite the most vigilant calendar management, however, the presidency remains a 24/7 position, in which a phone call may come in the middle of the night concerning a fire on campus or a student health emergency in a residence hall. It is not unusual to be stopped in the corridor by a teacher, a staff member, a student, or a parent with the lead question, "Do you have a minute?" Members of the community may seek to communicate with the president "off the record" or share information in a way that tries to "protect" the president from the true situation; others test personal boundaries or attempt to secure confidential information.[9] Many leaders liken their experiences to a "fishbowl" situation, and successful leaders learn how to navigate these waters, protecting the precious commodity of time and their own privacy in a gracious but careful manner.

Self-Reflection

High-impact leaders believe in life-long learning and are willing to reflect continually on their experiences. More importantly,

Qualities of High-Impact Leadership   125

they are willing to own and learn from their experiences—the successes and the mistakes, the triumphs and the failures—a disposition that requires a certain level of humility, a keen awareness of personal strengths and weaknesses, and an openness to change. Regardless of the level of responsibility, self-reflective leaders look for mentors and other respected resources as they seek advice and welcome help.

One immediate source of guidance is to study individuals who are widely regarded as great leaders.[10] What makes these people great? How did they achieve success? In what ways were they courageous? In a serious setback, how did they change their strategies and immediately address the crisis? How did they demonstrate grit and resilience?[11] How did they handle failures and mistakes? How did they express empathy and compassion? How did they inspire?

Historian Nancy F. Koehn offers the following analysis in her work, entitled *Forged in Crisis: The Power of Courageous Leadership in Turbulent Times:*

> Each of these leaders—Ernest Shackleton, Abraham Lincoln, Frederick Douglass, Dietrich Bonhoeffer, and Rachel Carlson—was thus forged in crisis. Intentionally, sometimes bravely, and with the messy humanity that defines all of us when we're at our most vulnerable, these people made themselves into effective agents of change. They worked from the inside out—*from within themselves*—making a commitment to a bigger purpose, summoning the courage to adhere to this purpose in the face of huge setbacks, and harnessing the emotional awareness to navigate the turbulence around them. They then used the internal assets and insights they gleaned about their own leadership to try to change the world in important, positive ways.[12]

While Catholic school presidents may not face the momentous historical challenges described in Koehn's research, they nonetheless face serious issues that have long-term consequences that impact thousands of people. By taking time to study the legacy of great leaders, present-day presidents can

126 *Chapter 6*

reflect on their own strengths and weaknesses with openness and modesty but also with a certain degree of confidence.

Leaders who are self-reflective examine their own gifts and talents, always within the framework of service to their school community. They confront their weaknesses and find ways to improve. When failure occurs, they examine the root causes and how they coped. Finding the answers to these questions, though the questions are often not easy to ask, leads to an honest snapshot of the current situation, along with possible avenues for improvement.

To that end, a high-impact president should also ask the question, "Do I take enough time to be self-reflective?" Most school presidents are bombarded with a barrage of appointments, meetings, presentations, personnel issues, emails, and reports, and it is simply too easy to get buried in the work, thereby eliminating quiet time for self-reflection. To offset this tendency, it is important to set aside some time each day to practice the discipline of self-reflection. For some this will occur early in the morning before the start of the professional day. For others it will be at the close of the workday or perhaps on a daily walk over the noon hour. The point is that the president should make the practice of self-reflection a regular occurrence in order to constantly improve his or her effectiveness as a leader. A leader who waits for the "annual senior administrators' retreat" or the "biannual board of trustees' professional development seminar" is missing the benefit of the immediate effects that come from the regular practice of self-reflection.

Self-Care

Presidents understand that no day is the same but that every day requires a high level of energy. They are "always on," regardless of the situation, which can vary from a student basketball game to a major black-tie fundraising event. People watch leaders, expecting them to behave in a way that is both dignified and approachable, even as the weight of responsibilities impacts their lives.[13]

Qualities of High-Impact Leadership   127

In order to "bring their best self" to the role every day, the president and all senior administrators need to take care of themselves by maintaining balance in their own lives, especially as their roles and responsibilities are stressful and require high levels of stamina.[14] Rest, reflection, exercise, vacations, a proper diet, and time with family members and friends—these all enhance a leader's overall well-being by establishing a healthy pace and rhythm in one's life outside the school environment. One highly respected president once stated that he was committed to getting sufficient sleep each night because his academic community always concluded that there must be something wrong at the school (finances, enrollment) if he looked tired or agitated.

A high-impact leader wants to bring their very best self to school every day. They want to succeed, both for themselves and for the sake of the school. High-impact leaders understand that they hold a unique role in projecting optimism and hope within their communities, even as they address institutional problems or are in the process of making serious decisions. For these reasons and many more, leaders need to address their situations honestly, especially if there are serious personal issues or illnesses (such as alcohol dependency or other significant addictions). Diseases only get worse unless they are dealt with forthrightly. Likewise, when experiencing a grave family crisis—for example, serious marital issues or a child's acute illness—the president should seek proper resources, including counseling (outside the school). These situations, if not properly addressed, can easily overwhelm a president's professional life and detract from the energy, focus, and strength needed to lead a Catholic academic community.

A Life of Faith

While all the qualities mentioned here are extraordinarily important for developing high-impact leaders, they alone cannot fully describe the qualities of the president who serves in Catholic education. A life of faith in God and commitment to

128   *Chapter 6*

Jesus Christ, combined with the regular practice of worship and prayer, are essential dispositions of the heart for those called to lead a Catholic school. Active participation in the Church's liturgical life, as well as the practice of service, are also necessary components of this type of leadership. Religious practice enables the president to be quietly attentive to the importance of the everyday moments, as Pope Francis often encourages.[15] It helps cultivate "an understanding heart," the gift that King Solomon requested when offered the opportunity to ask for anything he desired.[16] Such a disposition in turn strengthens and sustains the virtues of compassion, humility, and courage, as well as the ability to bring healing and unity to the academic community, especially in moments of crisis or great loss. Such a disposition also seeks clarity through discernment and prayer, especially regarding difficult decisions or amid experiences for which there is no script or carefully mapped path forward.

A life of faith and prayer gives deeper meaning to moments of great joy and sustenance during moments of trial, especially when decisions are misunderstood or not supported; they also heal in times of criticism or betrayal by a trusted community member. Moreover, a life of faith and prayer ultimately empowers the president to "lead a life worthy of your calling" and develop the type of strong character expected of a leader within a community of faith.[17]

How to Develop High-Impact Leadership Qualities

- Take steps to develop both-and thinking.
- Learn to anticipate problems and the possibility that Plan A may fail. Always have a Plan B.
- Never waver from the principles of integrity and authenticity.
- Embrace the unknown and a "what-if" mindset.
- Thoroughly consult within the community, then be decisive and confident in decision-making.
- Always work on improving communication skills.
- Manage time carefully.

Qualities of High-Impact Leadership 129

- Take time for self-reflection.
- Exercise self-care.
- Cherish a life of faith.

Key Questions

1. How do you describe your leadership style?
2. What positive qualities characterize your leadership style?
3. What leadership qualities do you hope to develop?
4. Think of real examples of the both-and creative tension that currently exist. How are you balancing the competing aspects? Are you comfortable with this type of tension?
5. Do you make opportunities for self-reflection and self-care?
6. Think of great leaders whom you have experienced or studied. What made them great? How did they inspire? How did they handle failure? Which of their specific qualities do you hope to emulate?
7. Do you consider yourself to be a decisive leader? If so, cite examples of situations when you demonstrated this quality.
8. What are your strengths in communication? In what areas do you seek to improve?
9. Do you see yourself as an innovative person? Cite examples.
10. Have you ever experienced the death of a faculty member, staff member, or student? How did you respond? How did you address the community, especially students? What did you learn about yourself from this experience?

Case Study: Qualities of Leadership

Early on a Monday morning, Ron and Cindy Johnson call your office requesting an immediate appointment to discuss a matter of urgency involving their daughter, Ashley, who is a junior in your high school. They refuse to reveal the urgent matter until they meet with you but do indicate that they have kept the entire

130   Chapter 6

day open in order to see you at a convenient time.

Your administrative assistant asks for direction in responding to the request, as your calendar this week is already full due to a board of trustees meeting scheduled for two days later. Last-minute requests to modify agenda items by certain trustees have led to extensive extra work in your office. However, parental requests to address urgent matters have always been one of your top priorities, and you agree to schedule the Johnsons' appointment for that same day at 5:00 p.m.

The Johnsons arrive promptly at 5:00 p.m. and are directed to your office. Both are somber and clearly upset as they recount what Ashley had disclosed to them about a certain well-liked teacher, Mr. X, who has served on the school's faculty for over twenty years. They state that on a field trip held that previous Friday, Mr. X made inappropriate, suggestive remarks to Ashley about her physical appearance. They fear that their daughter may have posted a video on her Instagram account, sharing the situation with her friends, but they do not want Ashely to get in trouble for the posting. They claim that Ashley's friends report experiencing the same type of unwelcome behavior on the part of Mr. X, although Mr. and Mrs. Johnson do not know specific examples concerning these friends' claims.

The Johnsons demand prompt action on your part but are not specific about what that action should be. Nevertheless, they state that they are prepared to go to the chair of the board of trustees and the media if the matter is not addressed immediately.

What do you say to these parents? Whom do you contact immediately after meeting with them? Is it necessary to speak directly with Ashley? Is it necessary to speak directly with Mr. X at this time? What other meetings do you need to schedule? Do you involve other administrators in those meetings? Should you immediately contact the school's lawyer? Do you involve the board chair and the communications director at this time?

List (in chronological order) all the steps that you will take to address this situation. How do you continue to prepare for this week's board of trustees meeting?

Identify all the qualities of leadership on which you will draw throughout this entire situation.

Notes

1. To cite a few, see Gardner, *Leading Minds*; Goleman, "What Makes a Leader?"; Keohane, *Thinking About Leadership*; Spillane, *Distributed Leadership*; and Antony et al., *College President Handbook*.
2. Gergen, *Hearts Touched with Fire,* 184–86.
3. Peggy Noonan, "How to Find a Great Leader," *Wall Street Journal*, November 3, 2018, A13.
4. For instance, see Goldsmith, *Obsessive Genius*; Isaacson, *Steve Jobs*; Shetterly, *Hidden Figures*; and McCullough, *Wright Brothers*.
5. Dierickx, *High-Stakes Leadership*, 171–73.
6. Noonan, "How to Find a Great Leader."
7. Finkelstein, "The Best Leaders," 142–45.
8. In chronological order: Kennedy, Commencement Address; US Embassy, "Martin Luther King, Jr."; White House, "Maya Angelou's Poem"; and "Queen's Coronavirus Broadcast."
9. Dierickx, *High-Stakes Leadership*, 72–75.
10. For example, see Michaelis, *Eleanor*; Roberts, *Churchill*; and Goodwin, *Leadership*.
11. Duckworth, *Grit*.
12. Koehn, *Forged in Crisis*, 7 (italics in original).
13. Bryant and Sharer, *The CEO Test*, 1–10.
14. Gunter-Smith, "Work-Life Balance," 291–96.
15. Pope Francis, *Encountering Truth* and *Reflections on the Sunday Gospel*.
16. 1 Kings 3:9.
17. Eph. 4:1.

Conclusion

SERVING AS THE PRESIDENT of a Catholic educational institution is a sacred trust and privilege, standing in a long tradition of leadership within a centuries-old tradition. Catholic education touches the very heart of the Church. It imparts the cherished belief that seeking truth within a faith-based context is not an artificial embrace of mutually exclusive realities, but rather is an authentic, attainable mission. Catholic education intentionally imparts this fundamental belief and understands that if the school does not thrive, the mission does not live.

High-impact leadership commits to developing and sustaining a vibrant Catholic school. While this mode of leadership accomplishes both immediate and long-term strategic goals in a relatively short time frame, it also commits to a community-based, collaborative model. If data-informed decisions, outcomes assessments, and solid, sustainable financial models are essential, so too are environments that foster moral values, student-centered teaching and learning, consistent communication, respect for the irreplaceable role of the faculty and the staff, and frequent expressions of gratitude for the sacrifices made by the parents, faithful alumni, and dedicated trustees.

High-impact leaders attempt to cultivate certain personal qualities, even as they realize that this personal growth is never complete; they are efficient and focused but they also appreciate a life of faith, prayer, and service. They strive to give their best

Conclusion 133

selves to the school community every day, even if that self is at times imperfect and a bit broken by mistakes and shortcomings.

However long one's tenure may be, a high-impact leader steps into the role and cherishes the countless everyday experiences, even as they keep their eyes on the broader educational horizon. As a self-reflective individual, a high-impact leader hopes to leave the school with a solid foundation for growth and in a stronger position than the one inherited. While one can never fully measure high-impact leadership, such a president will ultimately know success when the school community expresses its final gratitude with seven simple words: "You showed us who we could be."

BIBLIOGRAPHY

Abraham, Janice, Sarah Braughler, Liza Kabanova, and Justin Kollinger. *Risk Management: An Accountability Guide for University and College Boards.* 2nd ed. Washington, DC: Association of Governing Boards, 2020.

ACCU (Association of Catholic Colleges and Universities). "Trustees in Catholic Higher Education" program. https:///www.accunet.org.

AGB (Association of Governing Boards of Universities and Colleges). *Higher Education Governing Boards: An Introductory Guide for Members of College, University, and System Boards.* Washington, DC: Association of Governing Boards, 2019.

———. *Top Strategic Issues for Boards 2022–2023.* Washington, DC: Association of Governing Boards, 2022.

Antony, James Soto, Ana Mari Cauce, Lynn M. Gangone, and Tara P. Nicola, eds. *The College President Handbook: A Sustainable and Practical Guide for Emerging Leaders.* Cambridge, MA: Harvard Education Press, 2022.

Bahls, Steven C. *Shared Governance in Times of Change: A Practical Guide for Universities and Colleges.* Washington, DC: Association of Governing Boards, 2014.

Blackburn, Christine Crudo. "COVID Is Here to Stay." *Scientific American* 326, no. 3 (March 1, 2022): 78.

Breen, John M., and Lee J. Strang. "Academic Freedom and the Catholic University: An Historical Review, a Conceptual Analysis, and a Prescriptive Proposal." *University of St. Thomas Law Journal* 15, no. 2 (2019): 253–321. https://ir.stthomas.edu/ustlj/vol15/iss2/1.

Brown, Jessie, and Martin Kurzweil. *Instructional Quality, Student Outcomes, and Institutional Finances.* Washington, DC: American Council on Education, 2018.

136 *Bibliography*

Bryant, Adam, and Kevin Sharer. *The CEO Test: Master the Challenges that Make or Break All Leaders.* Boston: Harvard Business Review Press, 2021.

"Catholic Education on the Margins." *America* 227, no. 2 (September 2022): 12–13.

Chait, Richard P., William P. Ryan, and Barbara E. Taylor. *Governance as Leadership: Reframing the Work of Nonprofit Boards.* Hoboken, NJ: John Wiley & Sons, 2005.

Code of Canon Law, Latin-English Edition: New English Translation. Washington, DC: Canon Law Society of America, 1999.

Congregation for Catholic Education. *The Catholic School on the Threshold of the Third Millennium.* Vatican City: Holy See Press, 1997.

———. *Educating Together in Catholic Schools: A Shared Mission between Consecrated Persons and the Lay Faithful.* Vatican City: Libreria Editrice Vaticana, 2007.

———. *The Identity of the Catholic School for a Culture of Dialogue.* Vatican City: Holy See Press, 2022.

"Coronavirus Spring: The Historic Closing of U.S. Schools (A Timeline)." *Education Week,* July 1, 2020. https://www.edweek.org.

Cunningham, Lawrence S. "On Teaching Theology as a Vocation." In *The Challenge and Promise of a Catholic University,* edited by Theodore M. Hesburgh. Notre Dame, IN: University of Notre Dame Press, 1994.

Dacey, Stephen. "From Challenge to Opportunity: Positive Outcomes of Pandemic Teaching." *Momentum* 53, no. 2 (2022): 18–21.

Dallavis, Julie. "Centralizing Data, Monitoring School Vitality, and Building Data Culture: Best Practices from the Diocesan Data Study." *Momentum* 53, no. 3 (2022): 38–41.

———. "Fostering Parent Involvement in Catholic Schools." *Momentum* 53, no. 4 (2022): 40–42.

DeFlaminis, John A., Mustafa Abdul-Jabbar, and Eric Yoak. *Distributed Leadership in Schools: A Practical Guide for Learning and Improvement.* New York: Taylor & Francis, 2016.

Dierickx, Constance. *High-Stakes Leadership: Leading Through Crisis with Courage, Judgment, and Fortitude.* New York: Taylor & Francis, 2018.

———. *Meta-Leadership: How to See What Others Don't and Make Great Decisions.* Vancouver, BC: Page Two, 2023.

Drucker, Peter F. "What Makes an Effective Executive." *Harvard Business Review* 82, no. 6 (June 2004): 58–63.

Duckworth, Angela. *Grit: The Power of Passion and Perseverance.* New York: Scribner, 2016.

Bibliography 137

Dwyer, Judith A., ed. *The New Dictionary of Catholic Social Thought.* Collegeville, MN: Liturgical Press, 1994.

———. "Preparing for the Unthinkable." *The Presidency* 12, no. 1 (Winter 2009): 38–41.

Earl, Patricia Helene. "Building Catholic Identity Starts in the Hiring Process." *Momentum* 53, no. 1 (2022): 26–29.

Finkelstein, Sydney. "The Best Leaders Are Great Teachers." *Harvard Business Review* 96, no. 1 (January–February 2018): 142–45.

Fischer, Karin. "The Shrinking of Higher Ed: In the Past, Colleges Grew Their Way Out of Enrollment Crises; This Time Looks Different." *Chronicle of Higher Education* 69, no. 1 (2022).

Flannery, Teresa M. *How to Market a University: Building Value in a Competitive Environment.* Baltimore: Johns Hopkins University Press, 2021.

Galvan, John. "NCEA Rise: Grow What You Measure, Measure What Matters." *Momentum* 53, no. 4 (2022): 14–16.

Gardner, Howard, in collaboration with Emma Laskin. *Leading Minds: An Anatomy of Leadership.* New York: Basic, 1995.

Gergen, David. *Hearts Touched with Fire: How Great Leaders Are Made.* New York: Simon & Schuster, 2022.

Gleason, Philip. *Contending with Modernity: Catholic Higher Education in the Twentieth Century.* Oxford: Oxford University Press, 1995.

Goldsmith, Barbara. *Obsessive Genius: The Inner World of Marie Curie.* New York: W. W. Norton, 2005.

Goleman, Daniel. "What Makes a Leader?" *Harvard Business Review* 82, no. 1 (January 2004).

Goodwin, Doris Kearns. *Leadership: In Turbulent Times.* New York: Simon & Schuster, 2018.

Grawe, Nathan D. *The Agile College: How Institutions Successfully Navigate Demographic Changes.* Baltimore: Johns Hopkins University Press, 2021.

———. *Demographics and the Demand for Higher Education.* Baltimore: Johns Hopkins University Press, 2018.

Groome, Thomas H. *What Makes Education Catholic: Spiritual Foundations.* Maryknoll, NY: Orbis, 2021.

Gunter-Smith, Pamela J. "Work-Life Balance in the Presidency." In *The College President Handbook: A Sustainable and Practical Guide for Emerging Leaders,* edited by James Soto Antony, Ana Mari Cauce, Lynn M. Gangone, and Tara P. Nicola, 291–96. Cambridge, MA: Harvard Education Press, 2022.

Gyurko, Jonathan, Penny MacCormack, Marth M. Bless, and Jacqueline Jodl. *Why Colleges and Universities Need to Invest in Quality*

138   *Bibliography*

Teaching More than Ever: Faculty Development, Evidence-Based Teaching Practices, and Student Success. New York: Association of College and University Educators and American Council on Education, 2016. https://acue.org/wp-content/uploads/2018/07/ACUE-White-Paper1.pdf.

Hayes, Tom, and Doug Ruschman. "Marketing Research: To Outsource or Not?" *Currents* 48, no. 4 (July–August 2022): 35–38.

Heft, James L. *The Future of Catholic Higher Education: The Open Circle*. New York: Oxford University Press, 2021.

Holtschneider, Dennis H. "Treasure in Earthen Vessels: Bringing a New Generation into the Catholic Intellectual Life." *Journal of Catholic Higher Education* 40, no. 1 (2021): 20–34.

Hoyle, Michael. "If That Moment Arrives: The Blueprint to Close a College." In *Consolidating Colleges and Merging Universities: New Strategies for Higher Education Leaders*, edited by James Martin and James E. Samels & Associates, 199–208. Baltimore: Johns Hopkins University Press, 2017.

Isaacson, Walter. *Steve Jobs: A Biography*. New York: Simon & Schuster, 2011.

Kennedy, John F. Commencement Address at American University, Washington, DC, June 10, 1963. John F. Kennedy Presidential Library and Museum. https://www.jfklibrary.org/archives/other-resources/john-f-kennedy-speeches/american-university-19630610.

Keohane, Nannerl O. *Thinking About Leadership*. Princeton, NJ: Princeton University Press, 2010.

Koehn, Nancy F. *Forged in Crisis: The Power of Courageous Leadership in Turbulent Times*. New York: Scribner, 2017.

LeBlanc, Paul, and Kristine Clerkin. "A Disruptive Opportunity: Competency-Based Education as a Shaper of Successful Partnerships." In *Consolidating Colleges and Merging Universities: New Strategies for Higher Education Leaders,* edited by James Martin and James E. Samels & Associates, 123–35. Baltimore: Johns Hopkins University Press, 2017.

Lockdown International. "5 School Safety Measures that Have Changed Since Columbine." Accessed January 6, 2020. https://www.lockdown international.com/post/5-school-safety-measures-that-have-changed-since-columbine.

MacTaggart, Terrence. *Crisis Leadership for Boards and Presidents: Anticipating, Managing, and Leading Beyond Pandemics, Disruptions, and Ethical Failures*. Washington, DC: Association of Governing Boards, 2020.

Martin, James, and James E. Samels & Associates, eds. *Consolidating*

Colleges and Merging Universities: New Strategies for Higher Education Leaders. Baltimore: Johns Hopkins University Press, 2017.

———."The Consolidation of American Higher Education." In *Consolidating Colleges and Merging Universities: New Strategies for Higher Education Leaders,* edited by James Martin and James E. Samels & Associates, 3–13. Baltimore: Johns Hopkins University Press, 2017.

McClure, Kevin R., and Alisa Hicklin Fryar. "The Great Faculty Disengagement: Faculty Members Aren't Leaving in Droves, But They Are Increasingly Pulling Away." *Chronicle of Higher Education* 68, no. 11 (2022).

McCullough, David. *The Wright Brothers.* New York: Simon & Schuster, 2015.

McMurtrie, Beth. "A 'Stunning' Level of Student Disconnection: Professors are Reporting Record Numbers of Students Checked Out, Stressed Out, and Unsure of Their Future." *Chronicle of Higher Education* 68, no. 17 (2022).

Mellul, Corinne. *The Post–COVID-19 World of Work and Study: IFCU 2020–2021 Report.* Paris: International Federation of Catholic Universities, 2022.

Michaelis, David. *Eleanor.* New York: Simon & Schuster, 2020.

Miller, J. Michael. *The Holy See's Teaching on Catholic Schools.* Manchester, NH: Sophia Institute Press, 2006.

Morey, Melanie M., and John J. Piderit. *Catholic Higher Education: A Culture in Crisis.* New York: Oxford University Press, 2006.

NAIS (National Association of Independent Schools). *Trendbook: 2022–2023.* Washington, DC: National Association of Independent Schools, 2022.

National Academies of Sciences, Engineering, and Medicine. "Schools Should Prioritize Reopening in Fall 2020, Especially for Grades K–5, While Weighing Risks and Benefits." News release, July 15, 2020. https://www.nationalacademies.org/news/2020/07/schools-should-prioritize-reopening-in-fall-2020-especially-for-grad.

NCEA (National Catholic Educational Association). *National Standards and Benchmarks for Effective Catholic Elementary and Secondary Schools.* Leesburg, VA: National Catholic Educational Association, 2020.

Nicolás, Adolfo. "Depth, Universality, and Learned Ministry: Challenges to Jesuit Higher Education Today." Remarks at Networking Jesuit Higher Education: Shaping the Future for a Humane, Just, Sustainable Globe Conference, Mexico City, April 23, 2010. http://www.sjweb.info/documents/ansj/100423_Mexico City_Higher Education Today_ENG.pdf.

140 *Bibliography*

Orem, Donna, and Debra P. Wilson. *Trustee Handbook: NAIS Trustee Series.* 11th ed. Washington, DC: National Association of Independent Schools, 2022.

Pontifical Council for the Promotion of the New Evangelization. *Directory for Catechesis.* Washington, DC: US Conference of Catholic Bishops, 2020.

Pope Benedict XVI. Address to Catholic Educators at Catholic University of America, Washington, DC, April 17, 2008.

Pope Francis. "Audience with the Delegation of the 'Global Researchers Advancing Catholic Education Project.'" *Holy See Press,* April 20, 2022. https://press.vatican.va/content/salastampa/en/bollettino/pubbl ico/2022/04/20/220420e.html.

———. *Encountering Truth: Meeting God in the Everyday.* Edited by Antonio Spadaro. Preface by Federico Lombardi. New York: Image, 2015.

———. *Laudato Si'* (Care for Our Common Home) Encyclical Letter, May 24, 2015. https://www.vatican.va/content/dam/francesco/pdf/ency clicals/documents/papa-francesco_20150524_enciclica-laudato-si_en .pdf.

———. *Reflections on the Sunday Gospel: How to More Fully Live Out Your Relationship with God.* Translated by Matthew Sherry. New York: Penguin Random House, 2022.

Pope John Paul II. *Apostolic Constitution on Catholic Universities.* Vatican City: Holy See Press, 1990.

"The Queen's Coronavirus Broadcast." BBC livestream, April 5, 2020. YouTube video, https://www.youtube.com/watch?v=2klmuggOElE.

Regan, Bob. *Reflections on Catholic School Leadership, Governance, and Strategy.* 2nd ed. Boston: Carney, Sandoe & Associates, 2019.

Roberts, Andrew. *Churchill: Walking with Destiny.* New York: Penguin Random House, 2018.

Rose, Melody, and Larry D. Large. *Higher Education Business Models Under Stress: Achieving Graceful Transitions in the Academy.* Washington, DC: Association of Governing Boards, 2021.

Shetterly, Margot Lee. *Hidden Figures: The American Dream and the Untold Story of the Black Women Mathematicians Who Helped Win the Space Race.* New York: HarperCollins, 2016.

Smith, Annie. "Data Dive: Enrollment and Staffing in Catholic Schools." *Momentum* 53, no. 2 (2022): 48–49.

Snyder, Lincoln. "An Interview." Accessed April 5, 2023. ncea.org.

———. "The Journey Ahead." *Momentum* 53, no. 4 (2022): 23–24.

Soghoian, Richard J. *Mind the Gap! An Insider's Irreverent Look at Private School Finances and Management—with a Lesson for Government*

Bibliography 141

and Industry, Too! New York: Columbia Grammar and Preparatory School, 2014.

Spillane, James P. *Distributed Leadership*. San Francisco: John Wiley & Sons, 2006.

Temkin, Deborah, Victoria Stuart-Cassel, Kristy Lao, Brissa Nuñez, Sarah Kelley, and Claire Kelley. "The Evolution of State School Safety Laws Since the Columbine School Shooting." *Child Trends*, February 12, 2020. https://www.childtrends.org/publications/evolution-state-school-safety-laws-columbine.

USCCB (US Conference of Catholic Bishops). *Renewing Our Commitment to Catholic Elementary and Secondary Schools in the Third Millennium*. Washington, DC: USCCB, 2005.

———. *To Teach as Jesus Did*. Washington, DC: USCCB, 1971.

US Embassy and Consulate in the Republic of Korea. "Martin Luther King, Jr.: I Have a Dream Speech (1963)." Posted February 21, 2017. https://kr.usembassy.gov/martin-luther-king-jr-dream-speech-1963.

Vatican Council II. Gaudium et Spes (Pastoral Constitution on the Church in the Modern World). In *The Conciliar and Post Conciliar Documents, Vol. 1*. Rev. ed. Edited by Austin Flannery. Northport, NY: Costello, 1998.

Ward, William, and Mike Fassbach of NAEP (National Assessment of Education Progress). "NAEP 2022 Results for Catholic Schools." Webinar, December 15, 2022.

Wawzenek, Bryan. "Hear Me Out: The Art and Science of Listening Well." *Currents* 48, no. 4 (July–August 2022): 17–21.

Weinstein, Stanley, and Pamela Barden. *The Complete Guide to Fundraising Management*. 4th ed. Hoboken, NJ: John Wiley & Sons, 2017.

White House. "Maya Angelou's Poem, 'On the Pulse of Morning.'" January 20, 1993. Clinton Digital Library, https://clinton.presidentiallibraries.us/items/show/15928.

Wodon, Quentin. "Catholic Higher Education Globally: Enrollment Trends, Current Pressures, Student Choice, and the Potential of Service Learning." *Religions* 13, no. 8 (2022). https://doi.org/10.3390/rel13080735.

———. "Catholic Higher Education in the United States: Exploring the Decision to Enroll from a Student's (or a Student Advisor's) Point of View." *Religions* 13 (2022). https://doi.org/10.3390/rel13080732.

———. "COVID-19 Crisis: Impacts on Catholic Schools and Potential Responses, Part 1: Developed Countries with Focus on the United States." *Journal of Catholic Education* 23, no. 2 (2020): 13–50.

———. "Heterogeneity in Parental Priorities for What Children Should

142 Bibliography

Learn in Schools and Potential Implications for the Future of Catholic Schools." *Journal of Catholic Education* 25, no. 1 (2022): 178–205. doi:15365/joce.2501082022.

———. *Potential Impact of the COVID-19 Crisis on Catholic Schools and Universities: A Preliminary Assessment.* Paris: UNESCO Global Education Monitoring Report Team, 2021.

Woolhouse, Meg. "Catholic Schools Have Stayed (Mostly) Open During the Pandemic." *WGBH News*, February 25, 2021.

INDEX

Advent, 12, 13
All Saints' Day, 12
alternative educational models, 38
Antony, James Soto, 78
Ascension Thursday, 12
Ash Wednesday, 12
Association of Catholic Colleges and Universities (ACCU), 2, 14–15, 110
Association of Governing Boards of Universities and Colleges (AGB), 21, 84, 96, 110; and identification of top strategic issues facing academic leaders, 55

Baccalaureate Mass, 12
Barden, Pamela, 108
board of trustees/governance, 2, 40, 95, 110, 120; case study of, 112–13; critical issues facing a, 96–97; critical role of in revising a mission statement, 19, 24n13; executive committee of, 100–102, 121; finance committee of, 104–5; and fundraising, 105–10; governance committee of, 102–4; hiring a president of, 97–99; and the need to function in a high-impact manner, 100; successful collaboration of a school president with, 111; and succession planning, 104; and the trustee handbook, 102–3; valuing the role of, 82

Boston College, 15
Bryant, Adam, 41–42

Carr, Peggy G., 83
Catholic academic/school communities, 8, 16–17, 28–29, 105, 121; diversity within, 9; inclusive nature of, 9; leadership of, 1–2, 3. *See also* Catholic academic/school communities, fostering of
Catholic academic/school communities, fostering of, 48, 49, 69–70; by broadening student horizons, 58; case study concerning, 71–73; and the characteristics of a healthy school culture, 48–49; and the characteristics of an unhealthy school environment, 49; and the commitment to academic excellence, 53–55; by the creation of attractive environments, 51–52; by developing strong senior leadership teams, 63–65; by encouraging and assessing student participation, 57; by fostering safe environments for students, 59–61; by hiring those who support the enduring nature of the Catholic mission ("mission fit"), 65–67; by prioritizing employee professional development, 67–69; by prioritizing interaction with students, 58–59; by promotion of collaborative culture, 50–51; by promotion of

143

144 Index

Catholic academic/school communities, (*continued*)
parent engagement (both K-12 and college), 61–63; by promotion of student leadership, 56–57; by protecting students who may feel marginalized, 60; by providing substantive cocurricular offerings, 56–57; by recognizing the importance of ritual, 50; by recognizing the invaluable role of faculty and staff, 52–53

Catholic education, history of in the United States, 9

Catholicism, as a religion of mediation, 11

Catholic schools: and the creation of opportunities knitting an entire school through a single academic project, 54–55; and the impact of closing a school, 39–40; and strategic corporate alliances, 38. *See also* Catholic schools, K-12; Catholic schools, mission of

Catholic schools, K-12, 1, 2, 5, 33, 34, 54–55, 59, 81, 85, 107; changes in the educational approach of, 77–79; and the promotion of parent engagement, 61–62

Catholic schools, mission of, 8, 60, 62–63, 105, 120; mission effectiveness, 16; and "mission links," 9–10; and school hiring practices ("mission fit"), 65–67, 98. *See also* high-impact presidents/leaders, and the promotion of the centrality of their schools' Catholic mission (mission statement); mission statement, centrality of

Catholic social teaching, 14; enduring power of, 10

Cauce, Ann Mari, 78

Centers for Disease Control and Prevention (CDC), 80; concerns about the pandemic policies of, 93n5

CEO Test, The: Master the Challenges that Make or Break All Leaders (Bryant and Sharer), 42

Chait, Richard P., 95, 105

Clerkin, Kristine, 38

Clery Act, 94n17

competency-based education, (CBE), 38

COVID-19 pandemic, 31, 61, 83–84, 87, 94n10, 96, 101. *See also* COVID-19 pandemic, lessons learned from

COVID-19 pandemic, lessons learned from, 75–76; adopt a pastoral role, 76–77; concentrate on student wholeness, 77; embrace a steep learning curve, 80–81; focus on technological readiness and "best practice" pedagogy, 79–80; question a "normal" academic experience, 77–79; prioritize communication, 81–82; reexamine physical space, 82; value the role of the board of trustees, 82

Crisis Leadership for Boards and Presidents: Anticipating, Managing, and Leading Beyond Pandemics, Disruptions, and Ethical Failures (MacTaggart), 75

demographics, 33–35

Dierickx, Constance, 119

Drucker, Peter F., 3

enterprise risk management (ERM), 84, 85

Eucharist, the, 12, 15, 23

faith and reason, unification of, 8

financial analysis, for strategic plan, 35–39, 47n21; for a balanced operating budget, 36; for basic facility maintenance, 37; for evaluating investment managers, 37; for increasing endowments, 37; for paying off existing debt, 36; for seeking highly regarded financial auditing firms, 37; for technology maintenance, 37

Floyd, George, 94n11

Forged in Crisis: The Power of Courageous Leadership in Turbulent Times (Koehn), 125

Index 145

"Four Calls to Action" (Snyder), 54–55
Francis (pope), 14, 128

Gangone, Lynn M., 78
"generative landmarks," 105
generative thinking, 95
Georgetown University, 15
"globalization of superficiality," 13
God: gifts of, 12; manifestation of love in multiple ways, 11
governance. *See* board of trustees/governance
Governance as Leadership: Reframing the Work of Nonprofit Boards (Chait, Ryan, and Taylor), 95
Grawe, Nathan D., 34

Higher Education Business Models Under Stress: Achieving Graceful Transitions in the Academy (Rose and Large), 36
high-impact presidents/leadership, 3–4, 64–65, 132–33; and the inclusive nature of all Catholic academic communities, 9; leadership is not the same as management, 115–16. *See also* high-impact presidents/leadership, and the promotion of the centrality of their schools' Catholic mission (mission statement); high-impact presidents/leadership, qualities of; strategic planning process, opportunities and challenges for the president during
high-impact presidents/leaders, and the promotion of the centrality of their schools' Catholic mission (mission statement), 4, 8–9, 10–11; displaying the mission statement on the school's website, 11; placing the mission statement in key campus locations, 11; successful collaboration with a board of trustees, 111; through formal communications, 11
high-impact presidents/leadership, qualities of, 115, 128–29; "both-and" thinking creative tension,

116–17; case study of, 129–31; commitment to a life of faith in Jesus Christ, 127–28; decisiveness, 119–21; effective time management, 123–24; and the importance of communication, 121–23; and the importance of a Plan B, 118; and the importance of schedule dialogue for all constituencies of the school community, 122–23; innovation, 119; integrity and honesty, 118; recognizing leaders are public figures, 122; self-care, 126–27; self-reflection, 124–26; showing leadership when a student, faculty, or staff member dies, 123
human life: sacredness of, 10; value of, 14

International Federation of Catholic Universities (IFCU), 33

Jesus Christ, 8, 11, 128
John Paul II (pope), 2, 9

K-12 schools. *See* Catholic schools, K-12
Koehn, Nancy F., 125

Large, Larry D., 36
LeBlanc, Paul, 38
Lent, 12, 13

MacTaggart, Terrence, 75
Mass of the Holy Spirit, 12
Mellul, Corinne, 33
mission statement, centrality of, 21, 26; case study concerning, 23–24; role of the president in the centrality of, 21–22. *See also* mission statement, revision of
mission statement, revision of, 16–21; and the commitment to a community-based, collaborative process in revising the statement, 17–18, 19–20; critical importance of involving the board of trustees in, 19; formulating

146 *Index*

mission statement, revision of, (*continued*)
a complementary document to the statement, 18–19; inclusivity as critical to the process of, 18; as an opportunity for a school president to promote the qualities of a strong statement, 17; and realizing that "less is more" in drafting a revised statement, 18; recommended process for, 20–21, 24n14; as a sensitive topic, 16–17
moral values, 8, 10, 38, 93, 132

National Association of Independent Schools (NAIS), 110
National Catholic Educational Association (NCEA), 2, 14–15, 35, 110
National Center for Education Statistics (NCES), 34; effect of the COVID-19 pandemic on, 83
National Standards and Benchmarks for Effective Catholic Elementary and Secondary Schools (NCEA), 35
Nicola, Tara P., 78
Noonan, Peggy, 118

Office of Mission/Campus Ministry, 12–14; and the celebration of the Eucharist, Sacrament of Reconciliation, Prayers of the Faithful, Mass of the Holy Spirit, School Ring Mass, and a Baccalaureate Mass, 12; and the celebration of important Catholic days and liturgical seasons, 12–13; and the hosting of student, faculty, and staff retreats, 13; and mission-related professional development opportunities, 14–15; and partnering academic community members with existing social outreach programs, 13–14; responsibilities of, 12–14. *See also* mission statement, centrality of
"On Catholic Universities" (John Paul II), 2

planning process. *See* strategic planning process, case study of; strategic planning process, essential content areas of; strategic planning process, opportunities and challenges for the president during; strategic planning process, promulgation of
"Post-Covid-19 Era, The: What Future and New Presidents Might Consider" (Antony, Cauce, Gangone, and Nicola), 78
Prayers of the Faithful, 12

retreats (for students, faculty, staff), 10, 13, 15, 23
risk/crisis management, 83–89, 89–90; case study concerning, 91–93; and comprehensive risk identification and assessment, 84–85; details of assessing risk, 90; and developing strong relationships with community officials, 86; and enterprise risk management (ERM), 84, 85; and the need to avoid complacency, 85–86; as a top strategic issue for the AGB, 84. *See also* risk/crisis management, overarching principles for
risk/crisis management, overarching principles for: address crisis decisively, 87; build credibility within the community, 87–88; develop empathy and sensitivity for those impacted by a crisis, 87; develop a reservoir of inner strength, 86–87; plan a debriefing session, 89; possess humility in seeking advice, 88–89; release frequent and clear communications, 88
Rose, Melody, 36
Ryan, William P., 95, 105

Sacrament of Reconciliation, 12, 15
"school" defined, 2
School Ring Mass, 12
Sharer, Kevin, 41–42
Snyder, Lincoln, 54–55
Solomon, 128

Index 147

strategic planning process, case study of, 44–46

strategic planning process, essential content areas of, 32; addressing current challenges, 33; analyzing current demographics, 33–35; developing campus master planning, 39–40, 47n18; enhancing mission effectiveness, 32–33. *See also* financial analysis, for strategic plan

strategic planning process, opportunities and challenges for the president during, 41–42; the president aims high and develops a truly *strategic* plan, 27–28; the president clearly connects the process to the Catholic school's mission, 26; the president develops a future-oriented plan from the beginning, 26–27; the president develops a method for achieving tactical issues, 28; the president establishes a pre-determined amount of time for the process, 30–31; the president makes sure all constituencies have a voice in the process, 29–30; the president makes sure to avoid the "all-things-to-all-people" approach, 30; the president must keep the process simple, 31–32; the president must resist the temptation to project too far into the future, 30; the president must submit an executive summary of the process, 41; the president understands that there is no perfect strategic plan, 28–29; and use of the strategic plan as an institutional road map, 43

strategic planning process, promulgation of, 40–41; by developing a brief strategic planning document, 40; by developing an executive summary booklet, 40; by developing a highly detailed implementation document, 41

students: effect of the COVID-19 pandemic on, 76–77, 93n4; increase in student enrollment after the COVID-19 pandemic, 94n10; protection of, 59–61; student orientation days, 62

Taylor, Barbara E., 95, 105

teachers, 49, 60, 61, 65–66, 76, 79, 85, 87, 106, 117, 122, 127

teaching: importance of the quality of, 53; teaching methodologies, 53–54

technology enhanced active learning (TEAL), 39

Theology/Religious Studies Department, 15

Top Strategic Issues for Boards 2022–2023 (AGB report), 57, 96

truth, "collapse" of, 54

United States Conference of Catholic Bishops (USCCB), 2

University of Notre Dame, 15

Weinstein, Stanley, 108

Wodon, Quentin, 33

"world as a classroom" approach, 58, 74n1

Wright, Wilbur, 89

ABOUT THE AUTHOR

Judith A. Dwyer holds a PhD in theology from Catholic University of America and an STL from Weston Jesuit School of Theology. She has taught both undergraduate and graduate levels in several Catholic universities and served as an administrator at Villanova University, St. John's University (New York), and the University of Saint Thomas (Minnesota). At Saint Xavier University (Illinois) she served as president, and most recently she held the position of head of school at the Academy of Notre Dame de Namur in Villanova, Pennsylvania. She completed postdoctoral work at the Harvard Graduate School of Education, Northwestern University's Kellogg School of Management, and the Army War College. Throughout her career Dwyer, a former Fulbright Scholar, has promoted international education as a critical framework for all contemporary education.

Dwyer created and edited the award-winning *New Dictionary of Catholic Social Thought* (Liturgical Press), as well as several well-received titles with Georgetown University Press: *The Catholic Bishops and Nuclear War* (1984); *Questions of Special Urgency: "The Church in the Modern World" Two Decades after Vatican II* (1986); and *Vision and Values: Ethical Viewpoints in the Catholic Tradition* (1999).